English Solutions Book 4

Jim Sweetman

Shelagh Hubbard

John Mannion

English Solutions and the new GCSE syllabuses

English Solutions 4 and 5 meet the general requirements of the National Curriculum and the specific requirements of the individual GCSE syllabuses with a complete framework of differentiated activities. Students will practise speaking, listening and writing skills; study a range of texts; make comparisons between texts and comment on their social and cultural significance; and develop more complex reading skills.

English Solutions 4 The essentials of language meets the requirements of the GCSE English syllabuses at Foundation and Higher levels (covering the full range of grades) through:

- specialist units on standard and spoken English
- emphasis on reading prose, poetry and drama, and on writing in relation to purpose
- units that focus on the reading and writing of non-fiction, non-literary texts and aspects of the media
- texts from other cultures and traditions, many pre-1900.

English Solutions 5 The exploration of texts focuses on the closer study of texts as required by coursework and examination papers in GCSE English and English Literature. It does this through:

- the comparative study of texts
- reading within genre
- close examination of technique and style
- considering texts in their social and historical contexts.

Coursework

Both books encourage students to write in a range of forms and for different purposes. Carefully-structured activities take them through the process of planning, drafting and revising a coursework assignment and writing critically about modern and classic fiction.

Standard Grade and NISEAC

Materials included are appropriate for the Scottish Standard Grade examination in English and also for the NISEAC (Northern Ireland) syllabuses.

The GCSE syllabuses and English Solutions

NEAB

Unit 4 offers a poetry anthology for work on the NEAB anthology for English and English Literature.

Media study is part of coursework with NEAB. Units 6, 7, 8 and 9 will prepare a suitable unit for English.

Unit 5 will prepare for travel writing in English Paper 1 and lead to a piece of written coursework.

Units 1 and 2 are excellent starting points for the three assessed units in Speaking and Listening English coursework.

MEG

In Papers 1 and 3, MEG English sets unprepared non-fiction. Units 6, 7, 8 and 9 tasks practise these skills.

Units 10 and 11 support the Imaginative and Creative unit in English coursework.

Unit 2 explores the purposes for Speaking and Listening coursework for English.

Unit 3 is a pre-released exercise to match Section A of Papers 2 and 4 for English.

SEG

The anthology in Unit 4 is preparation for the English Literature anthology.

Units 3 and 10 practise the skills for English Paper 2, with a response to texts from other cultures.

Units 5 and 9 are a stimulus for the non-fiction personal writing in coursework. Unit 11 will help the writing of fiction for English.

ULEAC

Unit 7 mirrors the non-fiction in the anthology for Papers 2 and 4. Unit 4 provides comparable poetry.

Units 7, 8 and 9 offer media-based material for English Papers 3 and 5 exam preparation.

The short story in Unit 3 stresses the social, historical and cultural aspects required in the English and English Literature coursework unit on other cultures.

WJEC

The prose extracts in Units 3, 7, 10 and 11 are excellent preparation for English Paper 1.

Units 7 and 9 prepare for Paper 2.

The 'best writing' in English coursework should be carefully prepared. Units 8, 9 and 10 provide grounding and support.

There is more information on using English Solutions Books 4 and 5 with the new syllabuses in the Teacher's Guide. Remember that using the two books, plus a choice from the prescribed set texts, is a simple and effective way of ensuring that both the curriculum and the relevant syllabus requirements for English, and the additional requirements for English Literature, are fully met in a busy English department.

contents

Contents

contents

The activities in this book have been coded by colour, according to the *main* skill used in them. This coding is for ease of reference and does not imply that this skill is the sole focus of the activity; an activity coded a 'reading' activity may involve writing, and a 'speaking & listening' activity may often emerge from a reading activity and lead into a written outcome.

●	= Speaking & Listening
●	= Reading
●	= Writing

	Unit title and core activity	Development of key skills	Assignment	Language in use
a Speaking and listening	*Talking in public* **1. Speaking out** Exploring the features of persuasive talk through role-play, discussion, debate and the analysis of speeches by *John Major, Martin Luther King, Emmeline Pankhurst, Sojourner Truth, Nelson Mandela* and *Pandit Nehru*	● Contribute in discussion ● Listen carefully and positively ● Structure talk for an audience ● Note language change over time ● Engage with content and language ● Write in non-literary ways ● Use standard English	Role-playing using persuasive talk Arguing a case Reading and analysing public speeches Taking part in a class debate	Tips: **Persuasive talk.** Emotional appeals, entreaties, threats, conditional statements; personal, analogies, similes and metaphors, rhetorical questions, the 'rule of three'. Loud or soft voice, emotional tone, expectant pauses (page 9). Tips: **Kinds of argument.** The classical models: argumentum ad baculum, argumentum ad hominem, and argumentum ad populum (page 13). Lang: **Dialect and register in spoken language** (page 21). Tips: **Setting up a formal class debate.** The organisational skills needed, and the conventions of formal debating (page 22).
	Talking together **2. Advertising campaign** Working collaboratively to investigate how an advertising campaign is organised and presented	● Respond and restructure ● Reach conclusions through discussions ● Structure talk for an audience ● Respond to factual and informative texts ● Write in non-literary ways ● Use presentational devices ● Spell correctly	Discussing an advertising brief and naming a product Working in groups and pairs to repackage a product Designing a television advertisement, a poster and a leaflet Making a presentation to the class	Tips: **Writing slogans** for posters and other advertising (page 30). Lang: **Analysing written texts** with reference to subject matter, purpose and audience, the structure, tone, layout, vocabulary, style and register (page 31).
b Reading	*Reading prose* **3. The end of the trail** Reading a short story by *Garrison Keillor* and discussing the issue of smoking – responding in different forms of writing	● Contribute in discussion ● Respond and restructure ● Read narrative ● Engage with content and language ● Respond to factual and informative texts ● Write in non-literary ways ● Use presentational devices	Reading, talking and writing about a short story Rewriting a story from an alternative viewpoint Reading informational writing Writing and designing a leaflet	Tips: **Influencing readers' attitudes to characters** in your writing (page 40). **Producing a leaflet** - a step-by-step guide. Size and shape, layout, and the most effective form of presentation (page 42). Lang: **Leaflets and advertising posters.** Content, purpose and audience, layout style, text effects, illustrations (page 43). Tips: **Techniques for persuasive writing** (page 44).
	Reading poetry **4. Seven ages of woman** Investigating poetic form through compilation of an anthology of poems written by, and about, women and including writers such as *Elizabeth Barrett Browning, Grace Nichols* and *Liz Lochhead*.	● Respond and restructure ● Listen carefully and positively ● Note how language changes over time ● Read and respond to poetry including works by significant authors ● Engage with content and language ● Write in non-literary ways ● Understand the writing process	Reading Shakespeare (*Seven Ages of Man*) Reading poems, discussing their view of women and use of poetic structures and devices Arguing the case for the study of more poetry by women	Tips: **'Reading' poems** (page 49). Skills: **Similes and metaphors in poetry** (page 51). Skills: **Rhythm in poetry.** Irregular rhythm, syllables, end-stopped lines, enjambement (page 54). Skills: **Rhythm and rhyme in poetry.** Regular rhythm, iambic pentameter, rhyme schemes, limerick, sonnet and rondeau forms (page 56). Skills: **Repetition.** How it is used in poems (page 58). Skills: **Stanza length** (page 60). Skills: **Writing about poetry.** Revision of the terms covered in the unit, plus extended metaphors and similes, oxymoron, alliteration, assonance, onomatopoeia (page 65).

b | Reading

c | Writing

Unit title and core activity	Development of key skills	Assignment	Language in use
Reading non-fiction **5. Travellers' tales** Reading accounts of journeys by *Nick Sanders, Mary Kingsley, Mark Wallington* and *Maya Angelou*	• Structure talk for an audience • Understand the development of language • Read narrative • Respond to factual and informative texts • Engage with content and language • Write narrative	Reading and comparing four prose extracts Role-playing an interview with a traveller Writing about a journey	Lang: **Recognising formal and colloquial styles in writing.** Purpose and audience, vocabulary and form of address (page 77). Tips: **Role playing a television interview.** Strategies for the interviewer and interviewee (page 78). **Planning an interview** (page 78). **Planning your writing** (page 79).
Reading non-literary material **6. Qualified for work** Exploring reading strategies through the discussion of non-literary material about work and training	• Reach conclusions through discussion • Engage with content and language • Respond to factual and informative texts • Read poetry • Write in non-literary ways	Skim-reading a range of texts for information Scanning a range of texts to identify details Close reading a text Suggesting how to adapt a text for television	Tips: **Reading techniques.** Skimming, scanning and close reading (page 85). Tips: **Close reading.** Analysing and annotating texts (page 87). Lang: **The visual media.** The concepts of category, language, agency, technology, audience and representation (page 88). Tips: **Adapting written texts for television** (page 91).
Reading the media **7. The home of the future** Exploring the issue of technological change and the promotion of new products through the reading of a newspaper article and advertisements.	• Respond and restructure • Reach conclusions through discussion • Respond to factual and informative texts • Engage with content and language • Write in non-literary ways • Understand the writing process	Brainstorming and evaluating new technologies Discussion of newspaper article on technological change Analysis of advertisements Commenting on existing advertisements and designing one	**Writing a commentary on an advertisement** (page 97). **A glossary of advertising terms:** product, copy, target audience, emotive words, images, slogan, persuasive language, associations, weasel words, jargon (page 98). Tips: **Top 20 questions to ask about advertising.** Image, slogan, copy, use of persuasive language, register and style, the audience (page 99). Lang: **Nouns and adjectives.** Concrete, abstract and proper nouns, new nouns and how they are formed (page 100). **How to create your own advertisement** (page 101).
Writing to inform **8. Newspaper pages** Working individually and with a group to prepare pages from a school newspaper	• Contribute in discussion • Listen carefully and positively • Engage with content and language • Respond to factual and informative texts • Write in non-literary ways • Use presentational devices • Understand the writing process	Reading about, and answering questions on, how a newspaper is produced Writing pages and articles for a school or community newspaper Reviewing finished newspapers	**The language of newspapers** - a glossary. Editorial, flat-plan, photo opportunity, features page and masthead (Page 105). Lang: **Sentences and phrases** (page 108). **Writing a newspaper.** Drawing up a flat-plan, finding the stories, finding the photographs, writing and editing the stories, writing headlines, preparation for production (page 108). Tips: **Using desk-top publishing.** (page 111). Tips: **Writing journalism.** Using the 'journalist's triangle' to structure news stories (page 112).
Writing to report **9. Caring for the planet** Exploring the language of report writing through the issue of waste recycling, and writing an investigative report	• Reach conclusions through discussion • Structure talk for an audience • Respond to factual and informative texts • Write in non-literary ways • Use presentational devices • Understand and use standard English • Spell correctly	Reading articles and answering questions Role-playing different views in debate Writing a report from a specified point of view Presenting the report to an audience	Tips: **Report writing.** Purpose and audience. The techniques of report writing: research, evaluate, write up, recommend. Sections to appear within a report: the title, the findings, the conclusion, the recommendations, the ending (page 121). Lang: **Report and narrative writing.** Purpose, audience, structure and style (page 122).
Writing to describe **10. Pictures of people** Studying how writers develop characters, with extracts by *Toni Morrison, Hanif Kureishi, Bernard MacLaverty, Fay Weldon* and *Anne Tyler*	• Contribute in discussion • Listen carefully and positively • Read narrative • Write narrative • Understand the writing process • Spell correctly	Reading and comparing character descriptions Writing a commentary Creating a character	Tips: **Narrative technique.** The first-person and the third-person (page 129). Lang: **Connectives.** Prepositions, co-ordinating and subordinating conjunctions, adverbial clauses and phrases, pronouns (page 131).
Writing to excite **11. Tense times** Investigating how writing can be used to create tension with extracts by *Bram Stoker, Margaret Atwood* and *Sara Paretsky*	• Respond and restructure • Understand the development of language • Read narrative • Engage with content and language • Write narrative • Understand the writing process • Understand and use standard English	Reading and analysing build-up and climax Studying the way tension is maintained, through questions and commentary Writing an exciting story	Tips: **The structure of exciting writing.** (page 139). Tips: **The language of exciting writing.** Sentence length, use of the historic present, point of view, comparative description, understatement (page 142). **Writing a commentary on literary prose.** The writer's stance, the setting, the structure, language, and style (page 145). Tips: **Using quotations in your writing.** Layout, use of the colon, indentation, reference to source (page 147). Lang: **Descriptive writing.** How to use adjectives and adverbs, comparisons, punctuation (page 150).

Speaking
& Listening

Successful speakers know what they want to say and think about who they are speaking to before they open their mouths. Good listeners concentrate on what is said to them. They give speakers a chance to finish what they are saying and then respond to what has been said. In your English classes, you will have to show that you are a confident speaker and a good listener in a variety of situations. These situations could include having a discussion with your friends, being interviewed, making a tape recording, acting a part in a play or giving a talk to the class.

Language in use boxes:
Dialect and register (page 21)
Forms of writing – Analysing written texts (page 31)

Talking in public

Speaking out

Think of all the purposes for which we use speech. We speak to tell people what we want, to inform them of things they do not know, to ask for help, to express our own feelings and opinions.

This unit is about persuasive talk. We use persuasive talk to make other people do what we want them to do, agree with us or change their minds. As you work through the unit, you will learn about how language is used to persuade. You will practise the skills of argument and debate in speech and in writing.

What persuasive talk sounds like

With a partner, talk about the last time someone used persuasive talk on you. It could have been:

- in a school assembly (maybe somebody encouraged you to be more polite, or to support a charity);
- at home (perhaps your parents asked you to go with them to visit some relatives);
- with your friends (for example, someone may have tried to make you go somewhere, or to do something you did not want to do).

Read the list of persuasive techniques shown in the Tips box below. Note down any that you can remember being used on you. Who used them? What was the situation?

Compare your examples with the rest of the class.

... on features of persuasive talk

The strategies used	What people say
Emotional appeals	'Baby seals are being clubbed to death as we speak.'
Entreaties	'Please, please, support Year 8's appeal ... '
Threats	'Tell me who raided the tuck shop or you're suspended for a week ... '
Conditional statements	'If you want that bike for Christmas, then you'll do this for me ... '
Personal	'How can you refuse your best mate?'
Analogies	'Just like a good team, we must all pull together ... '
Similes and metaphors	'The school is like a barrel of apples. One rotten one can ruin them all ... '
Rhetorical questions	'Haven't you got anything better to do?'
The 'rule of three'	'I'm not just asking because you're a friend; I'm not just asking because you're here at the moment; I'm asking because you're the best person for the job.'
Loud or soft voice	Shouting loudly can be effective, as can switching to a very quiet tone of voice.
Emotional tone	Some speakers can cry on request. A 'choked' delivery can be very effective.
Expectant pauses	This is a useful technique that allows the speaker to wait to see the effect of words and allows the audience to think ahead.

2 Acting persuasively

> Improvise two of the following scenes with your partner. Take it in turns to act the part of the 'persuader'. Be ready to show your best improvisation to the class.

a Roles: two friends. One friend tries to persuade the other to tell his or her parents that he or she will be staying at the friend's house, so that they can both go to an all-night party.

b Roles: two friends. One friend has started smoking. The other tries to persuade him or her to give up.

c Roles: a teacher and a pupil. The teacher tries to persuade the pupil to tell him or her about a protection racket which some older pupils are using to get money from new pupils in Year 7.

d Roles: a teacher and a pupil. The teacher tries to persuade the pupil to come on a theatre trip that the rest of the group have agreed to go on.

e Roles: a parent and a teenage child. The parent tries to persuade the child to come with him or her to see Uncle Roger and Aunt Meg and their horrible children, Kevin and Natalie.

f Roles: a parent and a teenage child. The parent tries to persuade the child to do a pile of ironing, tidy his or her bedroom, or clear out the garden shed.

As you watch one another's improvised scenes, listen carefully to the language used by the 'persuader'. Note down examples of persuasive language.

Write a short playscript based on one of the role plays, including at least five different persuasive features.

At the end, write a commentary about your script, pointing out the techniques of persuasion. Explain how you think the different techniques help change the point of view of the listener.

Keep the final copy for your coursework portfolio.

3 Have an argument

To 'argue a point' is to present a convincing case for your particular position on a subject. 'Having an argument' does not involve having a shouting match. In an argument, you simply try to persuade someone else that your point of view is right and theirs is wrong. However, your listeners will be trying to persuade you of their point of view at the same time!

> Working as a group of four, choose a *subject* from the left-hand column below. Then, each choose a *position* from the right-hand column.

Subject	Positions	
Transporting live animals for slaughter	Position 1	Absolutely opposed. It is cruel and unnecessary.
	Position 2	It is acceptable over short distances or within the United Kingdom.
	Position 3	It's all right anywhere if the animal is properly looked after on the journey. They're only animals, after all.
	Position 4	Farming is an international activity. Farmers are entitled to get the best price they can for their products.
Nuclear weapons	Position 1	Opposed to all of them. They are useless as defence because no one will use them.
	Position 2	Although some countries do have them, that does not mean that we should have them.
	Position 3	We should stop any new countries developing them, but we have to have them to defend ourselves.
	Position 4	In favour of them, whoever wants them. There have been no global wars since they were first developed.
Smoking in public	Position 1	No one should be allowed to smoke in public.
	Position 2	Smoking in public should be controlled – there should be restricted areas in shopping centres and public places where smokers are allowed to smoke.
	Position 3	The place should define the rules. Smoking should not be allowed in restaurants or on public transport, but it might be OK in pubs.
	Position 4	Smokers have rights like anyone else. Why should people tell them what to do?

Prepare by thinking about your chosen position and the subject. Note down key points you could make to support your position.

Now, spend ten minutes having a spoken argument. Your aim is to persuade your group to agree with you and not to be persuaded to change your mind.

Record the arguments on video, if possible. Observe the arguments of other groups in your class, either live or on tape. Note down any persuasive techniques that you noticed people using.

... on different kinds of argument

A long time ago, when many people were unable to read and write, formal speech was the best way to communicate to the largest number of people. As a result, it was more important than it is today. University students even studied how to make speeches as a subject of their course. The name of this subject was 'rhetoric'.

Latin and Greek scholars analysed spoken argument and identified different kinds of argument. Four of them are explained below:

1 *Argumentum ad baculum*
Literally 'argument with a stick', this means resorting to threats to make people agree with you:
'If the government fails to act quickly, our supporters will have no alternative but to take militant action.'

2 *Argumentum ad hominem*
An argument directed at the person, not the issue:
'If those who oppose us had more than the brain of a flea, they would see that I am right ... '

3 *Argumentum ad populum*
An argument supported by popular opinion:
'Everyone knows that any other government would make you pay more tax than we do.'

4 *Non-sequitur*
An argument which comes to a conclusion that does not follow from what was said:
'We both have two eyes, a nose and a mouth. Therefore we are equal.'

Watch out for examples of these.

4 Analysing persuasive speech

People who know each other quite well use persuasive language which is informal and conversational. Slightly different techniques of persuasion are used in formal speeches, where a speaker attempts to change the opinions of a larger, unknown audience.

Before you do the next activity, read the Tips box on page 13 on different kinds of argument.

> The extracts on pages 15–20 are all from speeches. Read them aloud with a partner. Then, complete this chart with information from each speech. Half of the first one has been annotated and filled in to help you.

Who is speaking	Major	Pankhurst	Truth	Mandela	Nehru
To whom?	Audience of supporters				
Persuasive strategies used	rhetorical question repetition/(rule of three) analogy entreaty rhetorical question				
Examples or quotations	'I passed the bookstalls, and what do I see?' on word 'memoirs' comparing 'party' to a 'family' 'I want to hear the answers loud and clear' 'Aren't you fed up with people running our country down?'				

Speech 1 *Basic values*

This is an edited extract from a speech given by John Major, then Prime Minister, to the Conservative Party Conference in 1993. Mrs Thatcher had just published her memoirs, and Mr Major was going through an unpopular phase.

Madam President, as I walked through the Winter Gardens during this week, I passed the bookstalls, and what do I see? I see memoirs to the left of me, memoirs to the right of me, volley and thunder. Let me say right away I am not about to write my memoirs, not for a long time ...

This conference is a very great event in the political calendar, but it's something else as well. It's a family gathering, and like all families, from time to time, we have our squabbles ...

I'm not absolutely sure that everyone's caught up completely with the current mood of our party, so I'm going to ask you three questions and I want to hear the answers loud and clear so that no one can doubt where you stand. Aren't you fed up with people running our country down? ...

I think that many people, particularly those of you who are older, see things round you in the streets and on your television screens which are profoundly disturbing. We live in a world that sometimes seems to be changing too fast for comfort. Old certainties crumbling, traditional values falling away ... people ask, 'Where's it going? Why has it happened?' And above all, 'How can we stop it?'

Let me tell you what I believe. For two generations, too many people have been belittling the things that made this country. We allowed things to happen that we should never have tolerated ... Criminal behaviour was society's fault, not the individual's. Fashionable, but wrong, wrong, wrong.

He misquotes a famous poem, 'The Charge of the Light Brigade'.

An appeal to family values with the *analogy* of the Party and the family.

A *personal* appeal and *entreaty* followed by a *rhetorical question*.

He uses repetition, the 'rule of three', for effect.

We've increased sentences, built more prisons, recruited more police ... no other party would have done so much. But we know now, it was not enough. In many parts of the country, crime figures have risen remorselessly. We have tried being understanding. We have tried persuasion. It hasn't worked ...

If we let young people off with a caution, a caution and a caution, it is small wonder if they feel there is no peer pressure turning them to law and order, and they turn to bigger crime ...

John Major

Speech 2 *I have a dream*

This is an extract from a speech made by Martin Luther King in 1963. King was a leader in the Civil Rights Movement which was campaigning for equal rights for black Americans.

I have a dream that one day this nation will rise up and live out the true meaning of its creed: 'We hold these truths to be self-evident; that all men are created equal.'

I have a dream that one day on the red hills of Georgia the sons of former slaves and the sons of former slaveowners will be able to sit down together at the table of brotherhood.

I have a dream that one day even the state of Mississippi, a state sweltering with the heat of injustice, sweltering with the heat of oppression, will be transformed into an oasis of freedom and justice.

I have a dream that my four little children will one day live in a nation where they will not be judged by the colour of their skin but by the content of their character.

I have a dream today.

I have a dream that one day down in Alabama, with its vicious racists, with its governor's lips presently dripping with the words of interposition and nullification, will be transformed into a situation where little black boys and little black girls will be able to join hands with little white boys and white girls as sisters and brothers.

I have a dream today.

I have a dream that one day every valley shall be exalted, every hill and mountain shall be made low, the rough places will be made plains, and the crooked places will be made straight and the glory of the Lord shall be revealed, and all flesh shall see it together.

This is our hope. This is the faith that I go back to the South with. With this faith we will be able to hew out of the mountain of despair a stone of hope. With this faith we will be able to transform the jangling discords of our nation into a beautiful symphony of brotherhood. With this faith we will be able to work together, to pray together, to struggle together, to go to jail together, to stand up for freedom together, knowing that we will be free one day.

This will be the day when all of God's children will be able to sing with new meaning:

> 'My country 'tis of thee
> Sweet land of liberty,
> Of thee I sing:
> Land where my fathers died,
> Land of the pilgrims' pride
> From every mountainside
> Let freedom ring.'

When we let freedom ring, when we let it ring from every village and every hamlet, from every state and every city, we will be able to speed up that day when all of God's children, black men and white men, Jews and Gentiles, Protestants and Catholics, will be able to join hands and sing in the words of the old Negro spiritual, 'Free at last! Thank God Almighty, we are free at last!'

Martin Luther King

Speech 3 *I incite this meeting to rebellion*

Emmeline Goulden Pankhurst (1858–1928) led the militant English suffragists from 1903 until the outbreak of World War I. In 1912 she was arrested and imprisoned, together with 150 others, for smashing the windows of shops in London's most elegant streets, as well as the windows at 10 Downing Street. Within a few months, the state of the prisoners' health had been so weakened by hunger strikes and forced feeding that they were all released.

Emmeline Pankhurst gave the following speech at the Royal Albert Hall in London on 17 October, 1912. It was her first public address after her release, and in it she called for further militant action.

It always seems to me, when the anti-suffrage members of the Government criticise militancy in women, that it is very like beasts of prey reproaching the gentler animals who turn in desperate resistance when at the point of death ... Ladies and gentlemen, the only recklessness the militant suffragists have shown about human life has been about their own lives and not about the lives of others, and I say here and now that it never has been and never will be the policy of the Women's Social and Political Union recklessly to endanger human life. We leave that to the enemy. We leave that to the men in their warfare. It is not the method of women ... There is something that governments care far more for than human life, and that is the security of property, and so it is through property that we shall strike the enemy. From henceforward the women who agree with me will say, 'We disregard your laws, gentlemen, we set the liberty and the dignity and the welfare of women above all such considerations, and we shall continue this war as we have done in the past; and what sacrifice of property, or what injury to property

accrues will not be our fault. It will be the fault of that Government who admits the justice of our demands, but refuses to concede them ... '

Be militant each in your own way. Those of you who can express your militancy by going to the House of Commons and refusing to leave without satisfaction, as we did in the early days – do so ... Those of you who can express your militancy by joining us in our anti-Government by-election policy – do so. Those of you who can break windows – break them. Those of you who can still further attack the secret idol of property, so as to make the Government realise that property is as greatly endangered by women's suffrage as it was by the Chartists of old – do so.

And my last word is to the Government: I incite this meeting to rebellion! ... Take me, if you dare, but if you dare I tell you this, ... you will not keep me in prison.

Emmeline Pankhurst

Speech 4 *And ain't I a woman?*

Sojourner Truth (1795–1883) was born into slavery in New York State. She gained her freedom in 1827, when that state emancipated its slaves. At the age of forty-six, she felt that she had been called by the Lord to travel up and down the land speaking about the sins against her people.

She gave the following speech in 1851 at a Women's Convention in Ohio, chaired by Frances Gage, who also wrote the speech down (Sojourner Truth never learned to read and write). Many of the people at the convention had not wanted Sojourner Truth to speak at all.

Well, children, where there is so much racket there must be something out of kilter. I think that 'twixt the negroes of the South and the women at the North, all talking about rights, the white men will be in a pretty fix soon. But what's all this here talking about?

That man over there says that women need to be helped into carriages, and lifted over ditches, and to have the best place everywhere. Nobody ever helps me into carriages, or over mud-puddles, or gives me any best place! And ain't I a woman? Look at me! Look at my arm! I have ploughed and planted, and gathered into barns, and no man could head me! And ain't I a woman? I could work as much and eat as much as a man – when I could get it – and bear the lash as well! And ain't I a woman? I have borne thirteen children and seen them most all sold off to slavery, and when I cried out with my mother's grief, none but Jesus heard me! And ain't I a woman?

Then they talk bout this thing in the head; what's this they call it? [Someone whispers, 'Intellect'.] That's it, honey. What's that got to do with women's rights or negro's rights? If my cup won't hold but a pint, and yours holds a quart, wouldn't you be mean not to let me have my little half-measure full?

Then that little man in black there, he says women can't have as much rights as men, 'cause Christ wasn't a woman! Where did your Christ come from? Where did your Christ come from? From God and a woman. Man had nothing to do with Him.

If the first woman God ever made was strong enough to turn the world upside down all alone, these women together ought to be able to turn it back, and get it right side up again! And now they is asking to do it, the men better let them.

Obliged to you for hearing me, and now old Sojourner ain't got nothing more to say.

Sojourner Truth

Speech 5 *A time for healing*

Nelson Mandela (1918 –) was released from prison on 11 February 1990 by the South African Prime Minister, F W de Klerk: he had spent 27 years in prison. Mandela was an internationally respected figure and the main symbol of black resistance to the political system of apartheid. He was to play a crucial part in the lead-up to the first elections for all South Africans that took place in May 1994.

The elections were won by the African National Congress, of which Nelson Mandela was president. The following text is an edited version of the speech Nelson Mandela gave at his inauguration as President of South Africa on 10 May 1994.

Out of the experience of an extraordinary human disaster that lasted too, too long, must be born a society of which all humanity will be proud. Our daily deeds as ordinary South Africans must produce an actual South African reality that will reinforce humanity's belief in justice, strengthen its confidence in the nobility of the human soul and sustain all our hopes for a glorious life for all. All this we owe both to ourselves and to the peoples of the world who are so well represented here today. ...

We, the people of South Africa, feel fulfilled that humanity has taken us back into its bosom, that we, who were outlaws not so long ago, have today been given the rare privilege to be host to the nations of the world on our own soil. ...

The time for the healing of the wounds has come.

The moment to bridge the chasms that divide us has come.

The time to build is upon us. ...

We understand it still that there is no easy road to freedom. We know it well that none of us acting alone can achieve success. We must therefore act together as a united people, for national reconciliation, for nation building, for the birth of a new world.

Let there be justice for all.

Let there be peace for all.

Let there be work, bread, water and salt for all.

Let each know that for each the body, the mind and the soul have been freed to fulfil themselves.

Never, never and never again shall it be that this beautiful land will again experience the oppression of one by another and suffer the indignity of being the skunk of the world.

The sun shall never set on so glorious a human achievement.

Let freedom reign.

God bless Africa.

Nelson Mandela

Speech 6 *While the world sleeps*

Jawaharlal ('Pandit') Nehru (1889–1964), a leading member of the Congress Party, was the first Prime Minister of India. He had been educated in British schools and universities but was a fervent Indian nationalist and – with Mahatma Ghandi – one of the key figures in the country's independence from Britain in 1947.

The following are extracts from a speech Nehru gave in Delhi on 14 August 1947. He had had no time to write the speech, which was given without preparation and without notes.

Long years ago we made a tryst with destiny, and now the time comes when we shall redeem our pledge not wholly or in full measure, but very substantially. At the stroke of the midnight hour, while the world sleeps, India will awake to life and freedom.

A moment comes which comes but rarely in history, when we step out from the old to the new, when an age ends, and when the soul of a nation long suppressed finds utterance.

At the dawn of history, India started on her unending quest, and the trackless centuries are filled with her striving and the grandeur of her successes and her failures. Through good and ill fortune alike, she has never lost sight of that quest or forgotten the ideal which gave her strength. We end today a period of ill fortune, and India discovers herself again.

This is no time for petty and destructive criticism, no time for ill-will or blaming others. We have to build the noble mansion of free India where all her children may dwell.

Jawaharlal Nehru

Write a short commentary on any of the speeches, analysing the use of persuasion and rhetoric. Use the Tips boxes to help you.

Now, write your own short speech arguing your point of view on animal experiments, nuclear weapons or smoking in public. Make use of the persuasive strategies you have learned about in this unit.

5 Have a debate

Plan a formal debate. Choose a subject which concerns your English class at the moment. Give the speakers time to research the topic and prepare their speeches.

Run the debate along the lines suggested in the Tips box on pages 22–3. You could record it on video.

◎ Language in use

DIALECT AND REGISTER

Spoken language differs according to who is speaking and the context or situation in which he or she is speaking.

Speakers tend to speak with their own regional *dialects*. Regional varieties of English use words in characteristic ways that help you tell where a speaker comes from.

But people also speak in different *registers*. A register is a way of speaking that is appropriate in a particular situation. Imagine a rap DJ on the radio, a politician in the House of Commons and a sports commentator on television. The differences between *the way* they talk – not *what* they say – are differences in register. If you witness a fight outside school, you would talk about the same event in different registers, depending on whether you were describing it to your friends, your parents, the headteacher or as a witness in a court case.

Watch television lawyers or politicians to see a persuasive register appropriate to a formal situation. Contrast that with the informal register you adopt when you argue with your friends and the register you would use when arguing that a teacher was treating you unfairly.

I

... on setting up a formal class debate

You know how difficult it is to persuade people to agree with your opinions. Arguments are noisy, and the loudest voices and the strongest opinions often come out on top. Debates are an ordered form of arguing where people put their points in turn.

To hold a class debate follow these steps:

Step 1
Decide on a topic for the debate and word it as a *motion*. A motion begins, 'This House believes that ... ' or 'This House supports ...'.

Step 2
Choose four speakers:
A *proposer* and *second* support the motion.
An *opposer* and *second* oppose the motion.

Step 3
Choose a *Chairperson* to run the debate. He or she will introduce the motion and each speaker. The role also involves deciding who in the audience should speak, as well as keeping order when the arguments get heated!

Step 4
Run the debate like this:

- The Chair begins by welcoming the audience and the speakers. Then the motion for debate is introduced. The proposer is introduced and asked to speak *for the motion*.
- The proposer speaks for four minutes. All the speakers can use notes but should not write out their speech, or try to learn one by heart. New ideas will come up during the debate. All speakers will need to add notes while the debate goes on.
- Speakers should stop within the time limit. If a speaker continues for more than an extra half minute, the Chair should stop him or her.
- The Chair introduces the opposer who will speak case *against the motion*.
- The opposer speaks for four minutes against the motion. The opening section of the speech can be used to attack what the proposer has said.
- The Chair introduces the second for the proposition, who speaks *for the motion* for three minutes. The opening section of the speech can be used to attack what the opposer has said.

6 Evaluate the results

- The Chair introduces the second for the opposition, who speaks *against the motion* for three minutes. The opening section of the speech can be used to attack the views of the second for the proposition.
- The Chair asks the audience to give views from the floor. He or she allows people to comment on what has been said and to give their own opinions about the motion. He or she tries to make sure views on both sides are heard.
- The opposer has two minutes to sum up the case against the motion.
- The proposer has two minutes to sum up the case for the motion.
- The Chair reminds the audience of the motion and takes a vote. He or she asks for *those in favour of the motion to show* (raise a hand), then *those against* and, finally, *those abstaining* (undecided).
- Having counted the votes and conferred with his or her colleagues, the Chair announces the result to the audience. The usual form for this is: 'Those in favour, xx votes; those against, xx. I therefore declare the motion carried/defeated.'

Discuss the success of your debate. If possible, record the debate on video and watch the speeches. Which speeches worked well? What made them effective? What persuasive strategies did you notice speakers using?

on target

After working through this unit, could you:

- explain to another GCSE student some of the strategies used in persuasive talk?
- make your points more effectively in an argument?
- prepare a speech for a debate on a topic of your own choice?

Talking together

Advertising campaign

All advertisements try to persuade people to buy something
– a product. When the product is something people already use,
a successful advertising campaign must persuade customers that
this particular product is better than others like it. If the product is
something new, then an advertising campaign must convince
customers that the product will improve their lives.

 This unit is about running an advertising campaign.
You will work in groups to produce advertising
material, including posters, leaflets and storyboards.
You will then present your advertising campaign
ideas to the rest of your class.

Working as a team

Work in a small group.

Imagine that the group is the creative team in a major advertising agency. Your manager has been talking to one of the company's most important clients. He brings you a 'job start' briefing which looks like the briefing on this page.

The tasks your team have to complete include:

- giving the product a new name;
- repackaging the product – designing a label and a logo;
- designing a poster and writing a slogan;
- drawing a storyboard for a television advertisement;
- writing a leaflet to distribute in teenage magazines.

Decide which of these tasks the whole team will need to work on together, which can be done in pairs and which can be completed by individuals.

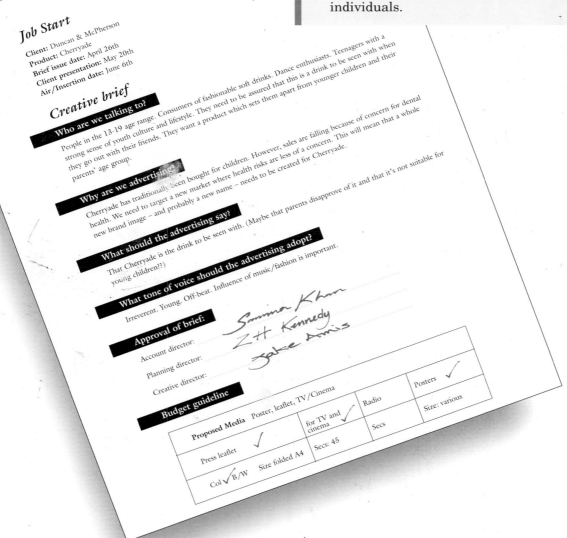

A K K

Amis Khan Kennedy

Job Start

Client: Duncan & McPherson
Product: Cherryade
Brief issue date: April 26th
Client presentation: May 20th
Air/Insertion date: June 6th

Creative brief

Who are we talking to?

People in the 13-19 age range. Consumers of fashionable soft drinks. Dance enthusiasts. Teenagers with a strong sense of youth culture and lifestyle. They need to be assured that this is a drink to be seen with when they go out with their friends. They want a product which sets them apart from younger children and their parents' age group.

Why are we advertising?

Cherryade has traditionally been bought for children. However, sales are falling because of concern for dental health. We need to target a new market where health risks are less of a concern. This will mean that a whole new brand image – and probably a new name – needs to be created for Cherryade.

What should the advertising say?

That Cherryade is the drink to be seen with. (Maybe that parents disapprove of it and that it's not suitable for young children??)

What tone of voice should the advertising adopt?

Irreverent. Young. Off-beat. Influence of music/fashion is important.

Approval of brief:

Account director:
Planning director:
Creative director:

Budget guideline

Proposed Media	Poster, leaflet, TV/Cinema	for TV and cinema ✓	Radio	Posters ✓
Press leaflet	✓	Secs: 45	Secs	Size: various
Col ✓ B/W	Size folded A4			

2 Find a new name

The name of a product can play a large part in influencing people to buy the product. The image of your product starts with its name.

Make a copy of a chart like the one below. Decide whether the product names are likely to appeal most to children, teenagers or adults. Try and give reasons for your decision. Do the names that appeal to your market group have anything in common?

Now, brainstorm at least five possible new names for Duncan & McPherson's Cherryade. Brainstorming means thinking of as many ideas as you can in five minutes. Decide which name will be the best.

Product name	Age group			What is there about the name that makes you think it is aimed at this age group?
	Children	Teenagers	Adults	
1 Curly wurly				
2 Gameboy				
3 Monster Munch				
4 Swatch				
5 Terry's All Gold				
6 Charlie Girl				
7 Nik-Naks				
8 Lilt				
9 Old Spice				
10 Hula Hoops				
11 Sprite				
12 Snickers				
13 M & Ms				
14 Cocopops				
15 All-bran				
16 Lynx				
17 Tango				
18 Quavers				
19 Mum				
20 Twix				

Repackage the product

At the moment, Duncan & McPherson sell Cherryade in large plastic bottles. The dark pink drink is the most noticeable thing about the product. It has a label which features cartoon cherries and bubbles. The colours used are bright pink and blue.

In your group, decide if this packaging will work for the new market group.

Discuss in your group:

- other methods of packaging – cartons, cans, smaller bottles;
- changing the colours used on the label;
- whether or not the actual drink needs to be visible;
- whether an abstract design, or even a photograph, would be better than cartoon images;
- the design of a logo.

Now, working on your own or in pairs, plan some new designs to go with your new product name.

Remember to:

- use colours that match your packaging;
- incorporate any drawings that will be part of the package;
- keep the logo simple;
- make sure that the name stands out.

Discuss these plans in a group.

Finally, on your own, draw a design for the packaging. Annotate your design to show what you consider to be its strengths.

4   Draw a storyboard

A storyboard like the one below is used to design a sequence in film or television where pictures, action and sound have to be synchronised.

Storyboards can be very complicated, including detailed timings and elaborate special effects. The one below uses photographs but many of them only involve very simple drawings or sketches. They all serve the same purpose of describing simultaneous actions and words.

MUSIC. (violin)

MUSIC. (violin)

MUSIC. (guitar)

MUSIC. (violin)

MUSIC. (guitar)

MUSIC. (violin)

MUSIC. (violin)

MUSIC. (guitar w/ violin)

"In a world of Choices"

"Pepsi"

"The Choice Is Yours"

"Harmony"
Versions Available

Brand	Supers	Code #	
Pepsi :30	w/s	PEIP 1003	(Stereo)
Pepsi :30	w/o	PEIP 1013	(Stereo)
Pepsi :30	w/s	PEIP 1313	(Mono)
Pepsi :30	w/o	PEIP 1323	(Mono)

Produce at least six storyboard frames showing the sequence of events in your advertisement. Make sure that you:

- create a link with your packaging and your poster;
- include a close-up of the product;
- repeat the name;
- use the slogan – maybe turned into a longer jingle set to music.

	1	2	3	4	5	6
Picture This shows what will happen on the screen. Use a variety of camera angles and close-ups.						
Action This gives instructions to the camera operator as well as describing what is happening on screen.						
Sound This gives details of music, sound effects and a script.						

5 Design a poster

A poster often starts with a slogan. Brainstorm in your group as many slogans as you can think of before reaching a decision. Think about what the words look like as well as what they mean.

Next, decide on the picture.

Your poster will mainly be used on advertising hoardings, so it needs to draw attention to itself. You have to decide whether the poster will:

- feature a picture of the product;
- show people drinking it;
- use ideas from the packaging.

On your own, design the poster. Include an eye-catching picture, the slogan and the logo for your product.

... on writing slogans

Remember that slogans can:

- be short;
- contain made-up words or made-up spellings;
- use alliteration;
- use rhyme;
- include the name of the product;
- depend on being printed in a certain way for effect.

Language in use

FORMS OF WRITING

Advertising is a particular form of writing with its own features. As a reader you can recognise an advertisement from the mixture of pictures and words, the short snappy slogans, the informal language and a variety of typefaces and colours. In the same way, if you are designing an advertisement, it is important to think about these features as you start to plan and write.

Other *forms of writing* include notes, diaries, personal letters, formal letters, chronological accounts, reports, pamphlets, reviews, essays, advertisements, newspaper articles, biography, autobiography, poems, stories, playscripts and screenplays. Forms of writing differ in a number of ways including:

Subject matter
The content of the writing. What is it about? Does it include a plot? Does it give information? Does it argue a point of view?

Purpose and audience
What is the writing for? To inform, persuade, entertain, argue? To be funny or serious? Who makes up the readership? Anyone, television viewers, children or the writer only?

Organisation
How is the writing structured? Is it chronological – describing events in the order they happened – or topical – describing information about a particular

subject? Is it argumentative so that points build up in order to make out a case?

Formality
Is the writing chatty and personal (colloquial) or 'official' in style?

Layout
Is the writing set out in paragraphs like a book, in columns like a newspaper article or arranged like an advertising brochure? Are headlines or sub-headings used?

Vocabulary
Is the choice of words very simple (as in a children's book) or very complicated (as in a book for specialists like lawyers or doctors)? Is the vocabulary factual (as in a news item) or descriptive (as in a holiday brochure)?

Sentence length
Are sentences long (as in a novel) or short (as in a leaflet)? Is the writing dramatic and designed to capture a reader's attention at once (as in a headline newspaper story) or more formal (as in a report on the causes of an incident)?

Use of language
Is there a lot of description or is the writing factual? Does the writing use jargon or technical words? Are these explained or is the reader expected to understand them?

Thinking about these features can help you as a reader and as a writer.

2

6 Design a leaflet

Design an A4 leaflet suitable for distribution in magazines read by your market group. The paper can be unfolded or folded – either in half, or into three. Remember that the layout and the style of language used in the leaflet must interest your market group enough to make them read it.

Your leaflet can include:

- pictures of the product, or ideas linked to your poster or cinema advert;
- the logo;
- the slogan;
- the copy (text) that aims to persuade your audience to buy the product;
- details of some kind of promotional offer – a money-off coupon, a free gift, or a competition.

7 Present the campaign

Finally, make a presentation to the rest of the class. Explain how your team intends to change the image of Cherryade.

Each member of the team should explain at least one of the decisions you made and present an example of the advertising materials you produced. Decide who will do what.

To help you:

- make OHP slides or flip-chart-sized examples of your ideas;
- prepare notes for what you intend to say;
- decide on the order of your contributions to the presentation;
- practise your presentation until it is really slick.

Make the presentation to the class. Take a class vote on which team would win the account.

on target

After working through this unit, could you:

- explain how an advertising campaign team makes decisions?
- work in a team to complete a design project in technology?
- write about how and why advertisements appeal to particular market groups?

Reading

A good reader is someone who understands what he or she reads and can respond to it in some way. You can show understanding by finding and comparing information, by appreciating characters, by discussing language and by reacting to arguments and ideas. In your English classes, you will have to show that you can 'read' in these ways. You will also have to read widely so that your reading record covers a variety of books, plays and poetry written at different times and in different places.

Language in use boxes:

Reading prose

The end of the trail

Smoking does not simply affect people who smoke. Scientific research has shown that it can injure those who live with, or come into contact with, smokers. So, should all smoking be banned? What would be the effect of this?

In this unit you will look at different types of writing on the issue of smoking. You will investigate writing techniques and different writing types.

The end of smoking

Read the following short story. It is set in America in the not too distant future. One section, containing some letters, has been omitted.

The end of the trail

The last cigarette smokers in America were located in a box canyon south of Donner Pass in the High Sierra by two federal tobacco agents in a helicopter who spotted the little smoke puffs just before noon. One of them, Ames, the district chief, called in the group team by air-to-ground radio. Six men in camouflage outfits, members of a crack anti-smoking joggers unit, moved quickly across the rugged terrain, surrounded the bunch in their hideout, subdued them with tear gas, and made them lie face down on the gravel in the hot August sun. There were three females and two males, all in their mid-forties. They had been on the run since the adoption of the Twenty-eighth Amendment.

Ames, a trim, muscular man in neatly pressed khakis who carried a riding crop, paced back and forth along the row of prisoners, their shoe soles motionless. 'What are you people using for brains? Can't you read?' he snapped, flicking the crop at their ankles. He bent down and snatched up an empty Marlboro pack and thrust it in the face of a pale, sweaty man whose breath came in short, terrified gasps. 'Look at this! This warning has been there for decades! Want me to read it to you? Want me to give you the statistics? What does it take to make you understand? Look at me! Speak up! I can't hear you!'

In fact, the smokers had been very subdued since long, long before the acrid tear-gas fumes drifted into their hideout, a narrow cave near the canyon mouth. They knew the end was near. Days before, they had lost radio contact with the only other band of smokers they knew of: five writers holed up in an Oakland apartment. It had been three weeks since the Donner group's last supply drop from the air, forty pounds of barbecued ribs, ten Picnic Tubs of Jimbo deep-fried chicken, and six cartons of smokes, all mentholated. Agents who searched the cave found exactly two cigarettes. There was not a single shred of tobacco found in any of the thousands of discarded butts. The two cigarettes were hidden in the lining of a sleeping bag, and the general disorder in the cave – clothing and personal effects strewn from hell to breakfast – indicated that some smokers had searched frantically for a smoke that very morning. Blackened remnants of what appeared to be cabbage leaves lay in the smouldering campfire.

'Move 'em out of here!' Ames said. 'They disgust me.'

Among the personal effects were four empty packs, carefully slit open, the blank insides covered with handwriting. An agent picked them up and put them in a plastic bag, for evidence.

The five smokers were handcuffed and transported to a federal detention camp in Oregon, where they were held in pup tents for months. They were charged with conspiracy to obtain, and wilful possession of, tobacco, and were convicted in minutes, and were sentenced to write twenty thousand words apiece on the topic 'Personal Integrity' by a judge who had quit cigarettes when the price went to thirty-five cents and he could not justify the expense.

The author of the letters was soon reunited with her children, and one night, while crossing a busy intersection near their home in Chicago, she saved them from sure death by pulling them back from the path of a speeding car. Her husband, who had just been telling her she could stand to lose some weight, was killed instantly, however.

Garrison Keillor (from Now We Are Married)

Answer these questions.

a Why are the smokers in hiding?

b What do the words 'a crack anti-smoking joggers unit' tell you about the America where this story is set?

c 'They knew the end was near.' Which details show their increasing desperation? What had they used the cabbage leaves for?

d Which words during the smokers' trial show that tobacco is now seen as a dangerous and illegal substance?

e What impression have you formed of the smokers?

f Do the non-smokers mentioned in the story – Ames and the judge – seem pleasant or unpleasant?

g Would you say that this is an anti-smoking story in its present form?

Below is the missing section from the story. It consists of letters from one of the smokers to her children. Read the mother's letters carefully and try to work out the meaning of all the shortened words.

They read:

Dear Lindsay & Matt –
This is to let y. know I'm OK & w. friends tho how this w. reach you I dont know. 5 of us are in the mts (dont know where). I never thot it wld come to this. All those yrs as ashtrays vanished fr parties & old pals made sarc remarks & FAA crackd down & smoke sect. became closet, I thot if I just was discreet & smokd in prv & took mints I'd get by but then yr dad quit & I had to go undergrnd. Bsmnt, gar., wet twls, A/C, etc. Felt guilty but contd, couldnt stop. Or didnt. Too late for that now. Gotta go on midnt watch. More soon.

Love,
Mother.

My Dear Children –

Down to 1 cart. PLMLs. Not my fav. Down to 1 cg/day. After supper. Hate to say it but it tastes fant. So rich, so mild. I know you never approvd. Sorry. In 50s it was diffrnt, we all smokd like movie stars. So gracefl, tak'g cg from pk, the mtch, the lite, one smooth move. Food, sex, then smoke. Lng drags. Lrnd Fr. exh. Then sudd. it was 82 and signs apprd (Thanx for Not S). In my home! Kids naggng like fishwives & yr dad sudd. went out for track. I felt ambushed. Bob Dylan smokd, Carson, Beatles. I mean WE'RE NOT CRIMINALS. Sorry. Too late now. More soon.

Love,
Mother.

Dear Kids –

This may be last letter, theyre closing in. Planes o'head every day now. Dogs in dist. Men w. ldspkrs. Flares. Oakland chapt got busted last pm. Was w. them on radio when feds came. Reminded me of when yr dad turnd me in. After supper. Knew he was a nut but didnt know he was a creep. Cops surr. hse, I snk away thru bushes. No time to say g-b to y. Sorry. Wld you believe I quit twice yrs ago, once fr 8 mo. I'm not a terrible wom. y'know. Sorry. Know this is hard on y. Me too. We're down to 2 pks & everybody's tense. Got to go chk perimtr. Goodbye.

Love,
Mother.

Dear L & M –

This is it. They saw us. I have one left and am smokng it now. Gd it tastes gd. My last cg. Then its all over. I'm OK. I'm ready. Its a better thng I do now than I hv ever done. I love you both ...

Answer these questions.

a   How did smoking become illegal?
b   How did the mother try to conceal her smoking? What drove her into hiding?
c   Why was smoking glamorous in the 1950s and 1960s?
d   What happened to the mother from the moment her husband turned her in until she was arrested?
e   What impression do you get of the mother? Does she seem like a terrible woman or a criminal?

With a partner, look at the story as a whole. Read it out in the order that Garrison Keillor intended.

● Discuss whether you now think this is an anti-smoking story.
● What difference do the letters make to your feelings about the smokers in the story?
● What else might the story be about?

2 Write about the story

The events of Garrison Keillor's story could be used to give a much more definite anti-smoking message if they were told from a different point of view.

> Re-write this story from the point of view of either Ames, the husband or the judge. As you plan your writing, imagine how these men might have felt about the end of smoking in America. Think hard about how they would have viewed the issue of smoking and the smokers themselves.

... on influencing readers' attitudes to your characters

 Choose your characters' faults carefully

For example:

In the story Ames is a bully, the husband is a betrayer and over-critical of his wife, the judge is mean. Although the mother is a helpless tobacco addict, she loves and even heroically saves her children.

 Allow characters to speak for themselves

For example:

The judge and the husband are only mentioned in passing. Ames has a larger part in the story but his words and gestures are cruel. The four letters allow the reader to get to know the mother best and see events from her point of view.

 Choose your words carefully

For example:

The husband is a 'nut' and a 'creep'. The wife feels 'ambushed' by the anti-smokers.

Write about the issue

The article below is taken from an American CD-ROM encyclopaedia. Read it carefully.

Burning tobacco

Smoking: inhalation and exhalation of the fumes of burning tobacco. The dried leaves of the plant are smoked in a pipe or in cigar form, but mostly in cigarettes. About 50 million people in the US currently smoke a total of 570 billion cigarettes each year. As recently as the 1940s smoking was considered harmless, but laboratory and clinical research has since proved that smoking greatly increases a smoker's risk of dying from several diseases, chief of which is lung cancer.

How smoking started

European explorers arriving in the western hemisphere observed native Americans smoking the leaves of the tobacco plant in pipes, and the practice was introduced into England in the mid-1500s. Most tobacco was consumed in pipes and cigars or as snuff. This pattern changed by the early twentieth century, when smokers were consuming more than 1000 cigarettes *per capita* each year. The general attitude of society was that smoking relieved tensions and produced no ill effects. During World War II, *physicians* endorsed sending soldiers cigarettes, which were also included in ration kits.

Epidemiologists soon noticed, however, that lung cancer – rare before the twentieth century – had increased dramatically, beginning about 1930. The American Cancer Society and other organisations *initiated* studies comparing deaths among smokers and non-smokers over a period of several years. All such studies found increased mortality among smokers, both from cancer and other causes. In 1962 the US government appointed a panel of ten scientists to study the available evidence. Their conclusions were included in a report, which stated that 'cigarette smoking is a health hazard of sufficient importance in the United States to warrant appropriate remedial action'.

The first action taken was the inclusion of a warning on cigarette packages. This warning was strengthened in 1969 to read as follows: 'Warning: The Surgeon General Has Determined That Cigarette Smoking Is Dangerous to Your Health'. A stronger sequence of four alternative warnings was developed in 1984. All cigarette advertising was banned from radio and television, starting in 1971. In the 1970s and 1980s several cities and states passed laws requiring non-smoking sections in public places and work places. In February 1990 federal law banned smoking on all domestic airline flights of under six hours.

How smoking affects health

Medical studies have established that middle-aged men who smoke are twice as likely to die young in comparison to those who do not. The death rate is higher for those persons who smoke more cigarettes per day and for those who have smoked longer. The American Cancer Society *estimated* that cigarettes were responsible for 148,000 deaths in 1988.

Smoking also causes a fivefold increase in the risk of dying from other lung diseases and a twofold increase in deaths from diseases of the heart and coronary arteries. A 1988 report based on a 26-year study of 4,255 residents of a suburb of Boston indicated that smoking increases the risk of stroke by 50 per cent – 40 per cent among men and 60 per cent among women. Other research has proved that mothers who smoke more frequently give birth to *premature* or underweight babies, probably because of a decrease in blood flow to the placenta. Three studies published in 1981 have suggested that non-smoking wives of smoking husbands experience an increased risk of lung cancer, and other studies have found

The end of the trail

increased illness in non-smoking children of
smoking parents.

Giving up smoking

Studies of ex-smokers show that their risk of
dying from smoking-related diseases decreases
with each year of abstinence. Encouraged by such
evidence, more than 30 million people in the US
quit smoking in the year following the 1964
surgeon general's report. The proportion of males
who smoke decreased from more than 50 per cent
to about 25 per cent; however, the percentage of
women who smoke cigarettes increased. Smoking
also became more prevalent among teenagers,
with about 29 per cent of high school seniors
admitting to smoking in 1977; but by 1987 this
proportion decreased to 18.7 per cent.

Many programs exist to help smokers quit.
However, more than 30 million persons in the US
say that they would like to quit smoking but
cannot. One *hypothesis* to explain this problem is
that the smoker craves the effect of the nicotine in
the smoke. In a 1988 report, the surgeon general
declared nicotine to be an addictive drug
comparable to other addictive substances in its
ability to induce *dependence.* The report also
called the monetary and human costs far greater
than those attributable to cocaine, alcohol, or
heroin.

Attempts are under way to help persons quit
smoking through counselling, participation in
support groups, and, for those with a strong
physical dependence on nicotine, substitution of
chewing gum containing nicotine to lessen
withdrawal symptoms.

Source: Microsoft Encarta 1994

Find out the meanings of the eight words or
phrases in italics and suggest an alternative
word or phrase to replace them.

Use the information to produce a leaflet
designed to persuade people to stop smoking.
Follow these steps for success.

Step 1
Decide on a size and shape. Leaflets present a short,
sharp message to a reader (see the Tips Box on
page 44). Start with a piece of A4 paper and decide
whether to:

- keep it as it is – to make a two-sided A4 leaflet;
- cut it in half – to make a two-sided A5 leaflet;
- fold it – to make a four-sided A5 leaflet;
- concertina it – to make a six-sided leaflet.

Step 2
Think about design. The layout of a leaflet is almost
as important as the choice of words. Think hard
about design and the headings you could use to give
your leaflet impact.

Step 3
Think about presentation. Leaflets are visual. Use
colour and print to make an impression.

Language in use

FORMS OF WRITING

A leaflet is a form, or a type of writing, with its own features. These features are sometimes called *conventions* and they influence how the leaflet appeals to a reader. The reader who picks a leaflet up recognises the form and therefore expects to receive a particular kind of message.

Using a familiar form alerts your reader to expect a particular message presented in a special way.

Posters are a form of writing similar to leaflets. So are the huge posters you see on hoardings and the advertising 'fliers' that come through the door. All have slightly different 'forms'. The chart below indicates the differences between the forms for leaflets and posters.

Form	Content	Purpose and audience	Layout	Style	Text effects	Illustrations
Leaflet	Advertising or advice	Selling or informing. Specialised interest groups or general readers.	Mix of print and pictures. A5 or A4 folded are typical sizes. Double or single sided.	Persuasive tone. Clearly presented information. Use of paragraphs. Slogans and sub-headings.	Different typefaces with varied sizes. Use of bold type for emphasis.	Usually more than one chosen for effect. Varied sizes but strong content.
Advertising hoarding	Advertising	Selling. General readers – passers-by.	Large. Mixture of slogan and image.	One large slogan. Persuasive – could be a question or command.	Large print for ease of reading.	Usually only one, linked to slogan to create powerful image and message.

Make a copy of the chart headings and complete the table for the following forms of writing:

- a letter to a younger nephew and niece;
- an article in *Just 17*;
- an entry in your personal diary.

... on presenting a message

 Write simply and powerfully
The facts you use should be clear and the emotions strong.

 Make facts and figures easy to understand
Graphs and charts are usually better than long sentences.

Comparisons give figures greater impact
Instead of saying '148,000 people died from smoking-related cancers' ask your readers to 'imagine two and a half Wembley Stadiums full of dead people'.

 Arguments should be simple
Mention one or two smoking-related diseases rather than the whole list.

 Be positive
The fact that 30 million people gave up smoking in 1964 is a better figure to use than to say that 30 million people want to give up now but can't.

 Appeal to emotions
The emotions that you appeal to might include:

- self-interest – no one wants to die before they have to;
- sex – cigarette smokers smell and are unattractive;
- respect for family values – parents who smoke can damage their children's health. Parents might die young and leave their families in trouble;
- social – tobacco-related diseases are a drain on the health service.

on target

After completing this unit, could you:

- write a story in which the characters support a 'message'?

- select key facts and figures from reference material?

- write a persuasive leaflet?

Reading poetry

Seven ages of woman

Ask anyone to tell you the names of some poets and you are likely to be given a list of male poets. Almost all well-known poets are male, even though women have been writing poetry for hundreds of years. It is only quite recently that their poems have been given much attention.

In this unit you will read and discuss poems written by women. You will consider how women's experiences differ from men's. You will learn about the techniques used in the poems and comment on some of the poems you have studied.

Mostly about men

Read the speech below. It is from one of Shakespeare's plays, written four hundred years ago.

All the world's a stage
And all the men and women merely players;
They have their exits and their entrances;
And one man in his time plays many parts,
His acts being seven ages. At first the infant,
Mewling and puking in his nurse's arms;
Then the whining school-boy, with his satchel
And shining morning face, creeping like snail
Unwillingly to school. And then the lover,
Sighing like furnace, with a woeful ballad
Made to his mistress' eyebrow. Then a soldier,
Full of strange oaths, and bearded like the *pard*, leopard
Jealous in honour and sudden and quick in quarrel,
Seeking the bubble reputation
Even in the cannon's mouth. And then the *justice*, magistrate
In fair round belly with good *capon* lin'd, large chicken
With eyes severe and beard of formal cut,
Full of wise *saws* and modern instances; sayings
And so he plays his part. The sixth age shifts
Into the lean and slipper'd *pantaloon*, clown
With spectacles on nose and pouch on side,
His youthful *hose*, well sav'd, a world too wide trousers
For his shrunk shank; and his big, manly voice,
Turning again toward childish treble, pipes
And whistles in his sound. Last scene of all,
That ends this strange eventful history,
Is second childishness and mere oblivion;
Sans teeth, sans eyes, sans taste, sans everything. without

William Shakespeare (from As You Like It, Act 2 scene 7)

With a partner, work out what Shakespeare is saying about the seven ages of man by making a copy of this chart. The first 'age' has been completed for you.

Stage of life	Appearance	Behaviour
1 the infant	with a nurse	being sick and crying
2		
3		
4		
5		
6		
7		

With a partner, make two similar charts for the seven ages of woman and man in our time. Are these different from the 'ages' of man in Shakespeare's time? Do the 'ages' of woman differ from the 'ages' of man?

Report back to the class.

Reading about women's experiences

Work with a partner as you read the poems in this unit. The tasks which follow each one of the 'seven ages of woman' will help you prepare for the written assignment at the end of the unit.

... on 'reading' poems

 Read the poem out loud – more than once.

 Discuss the meaning of words, lines and ideas you find difficult to understand.

 Discuss the questions or the issues raised in the poem.

 Read the skills boxes before trying to analyse the techniques used.

 Discuss how the techniques help communicate ideas.

The first age: *birth*

You're

Clownlike, happiest on your hands,
Feet to the stars, and moon-skulled,
Gilled like a fish. A common-sense
Thumbs down on the dodo's mode.
Wrapped up in yourself like a spool,
Trawling your dark as owls do.
Mute as a turnip from the Fourth
Of July to All Fools' Day,
O high-riser, my little loaf.

Vague as fog and looked for like mail.
Farther off than Australia.
Bent-backed Atlas, our travelled prawn.
Snug as a bug and at home
Like a sprat in a pickle jug.
A creel of eels, all ripples.
Jumpy as a Mexican bean.
Right, like a well-done sum.
A clean slate, with your own face on.

Sylvia Plath

In my name

Heavy with child

belly
an arc
of black moon

I squat over
dry plantain leaves

and command the earth
to receive you

in my name
in my blood

to receive you
my curled bean

my tainted

perfect child

> my bastard fruit
> my seedling
> my sea grape
> my strange mulatto
> my little bloodling

Let the snake slipping in deep grass
be dumb before you

Let the centipede writhe and shrivel
in its tracks

Let the evil one strangle on his own tongue
even as he sets his eyes upon you

For with my blood
I've cleansed you
and with my tears
I've pooled the river Niger

now my sweet one it is for you to swim

Grace Nichols

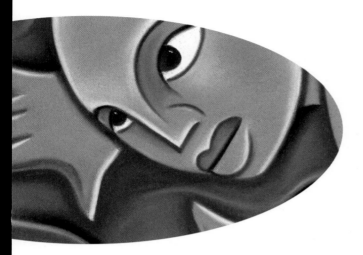

Issues for discussion

1   With your partner, discuss how the two
    mothers feel about their babies. Explain one
    similarity and one difference between their
    emotions.

2   With your partner, discuss where the mothers
    use comparisons to describe their babies. Make
    a list of the comparisons in each poem using a
    chart like the one below.

Skills Box

Imagery

A *simile* is a comparison which uses the
words 'as' or 'like'. A *metaphor* is a
comparison which says that one thing is
another. An *image* is a picture drawn in
words that represents a thought or feeling.

Sylvia Plath wrote her poem while she
was expecting a baby and shortly after
seeing some photographs of babies in the
womb. In the first stanza, she uses
imagery to show what her own must look
like. In the second stanza, she uses a
series of similes and metaphors to
describe her feelings.

Metaphor or simile	Meaning	Feeling expressed
Vague as fog	The baby is difficult to see or imagine	She is not sure what the baby will be like

3   Does the use of imagery give you a better idea
    of the poets' feelings about their babies than if
    they had written a literal description?

4   Explain what you think the final line of each
    poem means.

The second age: *lessons to learn*

Don't interrupt

Turn the television down!
None of your cheek!
Sit down!
Shut up!
Don't make a fool of yourself!
Respect your elders!
I can't put up with you anymore!
Go outside.
Don't walk so fast!
Don't run.
Don't forget to brush your teeth!
Don't forget to polish your shoes!
Don't slam the door!
Have manners!
Don't interrupt when I'm talking!
Put your hand over your mouth when you cough.
Don't talk with your mouth full!
Go to the market with me.
You spend too much money!
No more pocket money for you, dear.
Go to your room!
Don't stuff yourself with sweets!

Don't point!
Don't go too near the television.
You are not coming out until you have
    tidied your room.
Don't interrupt when I'm talking!
Did you get any homework today?
Always carry a pen to school.
Eat your dinner up.
Wear your school uniform!
Turn the television over to watch 'Dallas'.
Bring any letters home from school.
Come straight home tomorrow.
Tidy your bed.
Don't shout!
Don't listen to my conversation.
Don't look at the sun it could blind you.
Don't bite your nails!
Don't suck your thumb!
Why don't you answer me?
You never listen to a word I say!
Don't interrupt when I'm talking!

Demetroulla Vassili

The choosing

We were first equal Mary and I
with the same coloured ribbons in mouse-coloured hair,
and with equal shyness
we curtseyed to the lady councillor
for copies of Collins' Children's Classics.
First equal, equally proud.

Best friends too Mary and I
a common bond in being cleverest (equal)
in our small school's small class.
I remember
the competition for top desk
or to read aloud the lesson
at school service.
And my terrible fear
of her superiority at sums.

I remember the housing scheme
Where we both stayed.
The same house, different homes,
where the choices were made.

I don't know exactly why they moved,
but anyway they went.
Something about a three-apartment
and a cheaper rent.

But from the top deck of the high school bus
I'd glimpse amongst the others on the corner
Mary's father, mufflered, contrasting strangely
with the elegant greyhounds by his side.

He didn't believe in high-school education,
especially for girls,
or in forking out for uniforms.

Ten years later on a Saturday —
I am coming home from the library —
sitting near me on the bus,
Mary
with a husband who is tall,
curly haired, has eyes
for no one else but Mary.
Her arms are round the full-shaped vase
that is her body.
Oh, you can see where the attraction lies
in Mary's life —
not that I envy her, really.

And I am coming from the library
with my arm full of books.
I think of the prizes that were ours for the taking
and wonder where the choices got made
we don't remember making.

Liz Lochhead

Skills Box

Irregular rhythms

All poems have a *rhythm* – the beats of the words. Rhythm is counted in *syllables* – the sounds that make up the word. In some poems, the rhythm follows a set pattern with a predictable number of syllables in each line. In other poems, like these, there is no obvious pattern. The length of each line depends on the idea in it, and the words sound like everyday speech. An *end-stopped line* is where a whole sentence fits on a line; an *enjambement* (or *run-on*) is the technique of splitting a sentence into two, or more, lines of a poem. A poem can be written like this but still have rhythm.

Look at the way the lines in these two poems are organised. Does the mixture of long and short lines in 'Don't Interrupt' work well? What would have been the difference if all the lines had been the same length? If the lines of 'The Choosing' were end-stopped, what difference would this make? If all the lines were the same kind of length, what difference would it make to the poem?

Issues for discussion

1 With your partner, discuss what the two poems are saying about the influence adults have on children's lives.

2 Do parents and teachers have different expectations of girls and boys? Could the experiences described in these poems apply to boys as well as to girls?

3 Discuss whether there is a difference between what adults want for their children and what children want for themselves.

4 In 'The Choosing', find four or five places where the sentences are split over a number of lines. What effect does this have on the points the poem is making? What reasons can you find for breaking up the poem into separate stanzas?

The third age: *lovers*

How do I love thee?

How do I love thee? Let me count the ways.
I love thee to the depth and breadth and height
My soul can reach, when feeling out of sight
For the ends of Being and ideal Grace.
I love thee to the level of every day's
Most quiet need, by sun and candlelight.
I love thee freely, as men strive for Right;
I love thee purely, as they turn from Praise.
I love thee with the passion put to use
In my old griefs, and with my childhood's faith.
I love thee with a love I seemed to lose
With my lost saints, – I love thee with the breath,
Smiles, tears, of all my life! – and, if God choose,
I shall but love thee better after death.

Elizabeth Barrett Browning

Rondeau redoublé

There are so many kinds of awful men –
One can't avoid them all. She often said
She'd never make the same mistake again;
She always made a new mistake instead.

The chinless type who made her feel ill-bred;
The practised charmer, less than charming when
He talked about the wife and kids and fled –
There are so many kinds of awful men.

The half-crazed hippy, deeply into Zen,
Whose cryptic homilies she came to dread;
The fervent youth who worshipped Tony Benn –
'One can't avoid them all,' she often said.

The ageing banker, rich and overfed,
Who held forth on the dollar and the yen –
Though there were many more mistakes ahead,
She'd never make the same mistake again.

The budding poet, scribbling in his den
Odes not to her but to his pussy, Fred;
The drunk who fell asleep at nine or ten –
She always made a new mistake instead.

And so the gambler was at least unwed
And didn't preach or sneer or wield a pen
Or hoard his wealth or take the Scotch to bed.
She'd lived and learned and lived and learned but then
There are so many kinds.

Wendy Cope

Skills Box

Regular rhythms and rhyme

Both the poems on page 55 have the same *rhythm*. It is one of the most common rhythms in English poetry and is called the *iambic pentameter*. The iambic pentameter has ten *syllables* in each line, alternately unstressed and stressed (emphasised when spoken). You may recognise it from your study of Shakespeare's plays.

Rhyme is a feature of many poems. The *rhyme scheme* is a method of describing the pattern of rhymes in a poem. The first line is labelled A, and any further lines that rhyme with it are also labelled A. Where a new rhyme begins, it is labelled B, as are the lines that rhyme with it. The next rhyme is C, and so on. A *limerick* has an AABBA rhyme scheme.

A *sonnet* is a fourteen-line poem, usually about love. Traditional sonnets have strict rhyme patterns and are written in iambic pentameters.

A *rondeau* is a poem consisting of thirteen or ten lines with two rhymes. The opening words of the first line are repeated at the end, but do not rhyme. Wendy Cope's rondeau is called *redoublé* because it is twice the normal length.

Issues for discussion

With your partner, discuss how these poems exaggerate the good and bad experiences of being a woman in love. Both of you should use lists to do this.

1   Note down the list of 'ways' in which Elizabeth Barrett Browning loves her lover. What point is she trying to make about what true love is like?

2   Note down the list of things that were wrong with all of Wendy Cope's lovers. What point is she trying to make about 'true love'?

3   Give three reasons why Wendy Cope's message about love completely contradicts Elizabeth Barrett Browning's. Which poem do you think is nearer the truth?

4   Work out the rhyme schemes of the two poems. Why have these two poets chosen the difficult task of keeping to strict rhythm and rhyme schemes? Why are the sonnet and rondeau forms suitable for the subject of the poems? Which lines of these poems are *not* regular iambic pentameters? How does this help to emphasise certain words in those lines?

The fourth age: *work*

I had rather be a woman

I had rather be a woman
Than an earwig
But there's not much in it sometimes.
We both crawl out of bed
But there the likeness ends.
Earwigs don't have to
Feed their children,
Feed the cat,
Feed the rabbits,
Feed the dishwasher.
They don't need
Clean sheets,
Clean clothes,
Clean carpets,
A clean bill of health.
They just rummage about
In chrysanthemums.
No one expects them
To have their
Teetotal, vegetarian
Mothers-in-law
To stay for Christmas.
Or to feel a secret thrill
At the thought of extending the kitchen.
Earwigs can snap their pincers at life
And scurry about being quite irresponsible.
They enjoy an undeserved reputation
Which frightens the boldest child.
Next time I feel hysterical
I'll bite a hole in a dahlia.

Daphne Schiller

From: Six poems for hospital workers

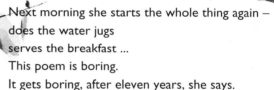

This is a poem for
the hospital orderly
who does the water jugs
serves the breakfast
serves the tea
gives out the menus
serves the coffee
cleans the lockers
collects the menus
serves the lunch
serves the tea
serves some more tea
and clocks off
Next morning she starts the whole thing again –
does the water jugs
serves the breakfast ...
This poem is boring.
It gets boring, after eleven years, she says.

This is not a woolworths waitress
(or is it)
This is a nurse in
the new national uniform
Little boy blue gingham and
a paper hat.
She gets electric shocks making the
new king fund beds.
Changing babies nappies would be better
she thinks, stowing disposable bed pans
at least they don't shit so much
all at once

Cleaning under this bed is
the married woman sociology student
who is working all through her vacations
as she doesn't get a grant
(her husband works all through his vacations
as a porter
and gets 30% more)
She has noticed with excitement

how nobody looks at cleaning women
or respects them
Nobody looks at students pretending
to be cleaning women either
(they don't join unions)
Everyone notices her accent
She talks loudly because her husband never listens
'Aren't you rather educated to be a cleaner, cleaner?'
they ask her constantly.
'Oh, you're a student.'
She's going to put it all in her dissertation.
She can't imagine how people who
work there always
put up with it
She gave in her notice today, gratefully
after ten weeks

Here is a poem for
the women who don't write poems
who do the work because work is
and do more work because work is
who are: fast, kind, vacant, fat
service and produce, produce and service
There are no words to write this poem because
they have no words.
Who would do their jobs
if they had words. No more words. The poem's over.

Diana Scott

Skills Box

Repetition

Both these poems use the technique of *repetition*.

Repeated words, phrases or sentence structures are used in a poem:
- to emphasise a point;
- to suggest that something is done often, or goes on for a long time;
- to suggest that something is monotonous.

Issues for discussion

1   With your partner, discuss the differences and similarities in these descriptions of 'women's work'.

2   With your partner, discuss the way that both poems end by comparing the lives of working women with another kind of life. What is it? Are these poems making a serious point? What is it?

3   Do you think the message of these poems is still true for young women growing up in the 1990s?

4   Look carefully at the lists in each poem. What kind of activities are described? Why have these poets chosen to use lists in their poems about work? Look at the final line of each of Daphne Schiller's lists. How are these different from the earlier items on each list?

The fifth age:
respectable middle age

Woman enough

Because my grandmother's hours
were apple cakes baking,
& dust motes gathering,
& linens yellowing
& seams and hems
inevitably unravelling –
I almost never keep house –
though really I *like* houses
& wish I had a clean one.

Because my mother's minutes
were sucked into the roar
of the vacuum cleaner,
because she waltzed with the washer-dryer
& tore her hair waiting for repairmen –
I send out my laundry,
& live in a dusty house,
though really I *like* clean houses
as well as anyone.

I am woman enough
to love the kneading of bread
as much as the feel
of typewriter keys
under my fingers –
springy, springy.
& the smell of clean laundry
& simmering soup
are almost as dear to me
as the smell of paper and ink.

I wish there were not a choice;
I wish I could be two women.
I wish the days could be longer.
But they are short.

So I write while
the dust piles up.

Erica Jong

The fat black
woman goes shopping

Shopping in London winter
is a real drag for the fat black woman
going from store to store
in search of accommodating clothes
and de weather so cold

Look at the frozen thin mannequins
fixing her with grin
and de pretty face salesgals
exchanging slimming glances
thinking she don't notice

Lord is aggravating

Nothing soft and bright and billowing
to flow like breezy sunlight
when she walking

The fat black woman curses in Swahili/Yoruba
and nation language under her breathing
all this journeying and journeying

The fat black woman could only conclude
that when it came to fashion
the choice is lean

Nothing much beyond size 14

Grace Nichols

Seven ages of woman

Skills Box

Stanza length

In a rhyming poem, each section is called a *verse*. A *stanza* is a section in a poem that does not necessarily rhyme. These two poems vary the length of their stanzas to help achieve their effects.

Issues for discussion

1   Make a copy of the chart below. Complete it to show the differences between what Erica Jong and 'the fat black woman' are *really* like and how other people expect them to be.

What Erica Jong is really like	How other people see her	What the fat black woman is really like	How other people see her

2   How do Erica Jong and 'the fat black woman' feel about not fitting in with stereotypes of respectability?

3   In small groups, prepare a reading of one of these poems for the rest of the class. Think about how the line and stanza length help you to decide how to read out the poem. What do you do when you come to a short line or stanza? Why do you think Erica Jong and Grace Nichols wanted these particular parts of the poems to stand out from the rest?

The sixth age: *growing old*

Warning

When I am an old woman I shall wear purple
With a red hat which doesn't go, and doesn't suit me,
And I shall spend my pension on brandy and summer gloves
And satin sandals, and say we've no money for butter.
I shall sit down on the pavement when I'm tired
And gobble up samples in shops and press alarm bells
And run my stick along the public railings
And make up for the sobriety of my youth.
I shall go in my slippers in the rain
And pick the flowers in other people's gardens
And learn to spit.

You can wear terrible shirts and grow more fat
And eat three pounds of sausages at a go
Or only bread and pickle for a week
And hoard pens and pencils and beermats and things in boxes.

But now we must have clothes that keep us dry
And pay our rent and not swear in the street
And set a good example for the children.
We will have friends to dinner and read the papers.
But maybe I ought to practise a little now?
So people who know me are not too shocked and surprised
When suddenly I am old and start to wear purple.

Jenny Joseph

I am becoming my mother

Yellow/brown woman
fingers smelling always of onions

My mother raises rare blooms
and waters them with tea
her birth waters sang like rivers
my mother is now me

My mother had a linen dress
the colour of the sky
and stored lace and damask tablecloths
to pull shame out of her eye.

I am becoming my mother
brown/yellow woman
fingers smelling always of onions.

Lorna Goodison

Issues for discussion

1   With your partner, discuss how Jenny Joseph's poem challenges stereotyped ideas of how an older woman should behave. As you do this, compare Jenny Joseph's hopes for old age with the kind of life Lorna Goodison sees herself leading as she becomes older.

2   Which of these poems seems more optimistic? Which seems more true?

3   Both of these poems use lists of things the two women wear, own or do. Make a copy of the chart below to note these facts. Discuss how the items you have listed help you to build up an impression of the characters of the two women.

	Wears?	Owns?	Does?
Jenny Joseph			
Lorna Goodison's mother			

The seventh age:
reaching the end

Passing and glassing

All things that pass
Are woman's looking-glass;
They show her how her bloom must fade,
And she herself be laid
With withered roses in the shade;
With withered roses and the fallen peach,
Unlovely, out of reach
Of summer joy that was.

All things that pass
Are woman's tiring-glass;
The faded lavender is sweet,
Sweet the dead violet
Culled and laid by and cared for yet;
The dried-up violets and dried lavender
Still sweet, may comfort her,
Nor need she cry Alas!

All things that pass
Are wisdom's looking-glass;
Being full of hope and fear, and still
Brimful of good or ill,
According to our work and will;
For there is nothing new beneath the sun;
Our doings have been done,
And that which shall be was.

Christina Rossetti

A crabbit old woman

What do you see, nurses,
What do you see?
Are you thinking
When you're looking at me
A crabbit old woman
Not very wise
Uncertain of habit
With far away eyes.
Who dribbles her food
and makes no reply
When you say in a loud voice
'I do wish you'd try'.
Who seems not to notice
The things that you do.
And forever is losing
a stocking or shoe,
Who unresisting or not
Lets you do as you will
With bathing and feeding
The long day to fill.
Is that what you are thinking
is that what you see?
Then open your eyes, nurses
you are not looking at me.
I'll tell you who I am
as I sit here so still
As I use at your bidding
The long day to fill
I'm a small child of ten
with a father and mother
Brothers and sisters
who love one another
A young girl of sixteen
with wings on her feet
Dreaming that soon now
a young man she'll meet
A bride soon at twenty
my heart gives a leap

Remembering the vows
that I've promised to keep.
At twenty-five now
I have young of my own
Who need me to build
a secure, happy home.
A woman of thirty
my young now grow fast
Bound to each other
with ties that should last.
At forty my young sons
now grown will soon be gone
But my man stays beside me
to see I don't mourn.
At fifty once more
babies play round my knee
Again we know children
my loved one and me
Dark days are upon me
my husband is dead
I look at the future
I shudder with dread
For my young are all busy
rearing young of their own
And I think of the years
and the love I have known
I'm an old woman now
and nature is cruel
'tis her jest to make
old age look like a fool
The body it crumbles
grace and vigour depart
There now is a stone

Where I once had a heart.
But inside this old carcass
a young girl still dwells
And now and again
my battered heart swells
I remember the joys
I remember the pain
And I'm loving and living
life over again.
I think of the years
all too few – gone too fast
And accept the stark fact
that nothing can last.
So open your eyes, nurses,
open and see
Not a crabbit old woman
look closer – see ME.

Anonymous

Issues for discussion

1 With your partner, discuss how Christina Rossetti's slight changes to the words of the second line of each stanza help to introduce us to the losses and gains of growing very old.

2 Discuss why the title of 'A crabbit old woman' turns out to be ironic. What is the poem trying to tell us about judging very old people by their appearance?

3 What similarities are there between the messages of these two poems?

4 Work out the rhyme schemes of these two poems. Discuss the way rhyme patterns help to break a poem up into chunks of meaning – like paragraphs in a story.

◎ Language in use

Writing about poetry

This unit has discussed all the following terms. Make sure you know what they mean and how to apply them to your reading.

image   metaphor   repetition   rhyme
rhythm   simile   sonnet   stanza   verse

Other terms you should know when talking or writing about poetry include:

extended metaphor ⎫ where a comparison is
extended similes ⎬ continued over a
　　　　　　　　 ⎭ number of lines

oxymoron where words that are opposite in meaning are put together for effect

alliteration the repetition of letters or sounds at the start of words

assonance the use of groups of words to conjure up sounds

onomatopoeia the use of individual words whose sound symbolises, or stands for, their meaning

4

3 Why study women's poetry?

Why is most published poetry written by men? Join up with another pair and discuss why there are far more poems written by men than by women in most anthologies.

Here are some reasons that have been given for the fact that so little published poetry is by women. People have said that women's poetry is:

- difficult to find because men write more;
- not as good as men's poetry;
- not about important or exciting things, like war, politics or disasters;
- about soppy things like babies, nature and love;
- about trivial things like clothes and housework;
- not as popular as men's poetry – so publishers won't make much money from it;
- about personal, private things that only women would be interested in;
- not important enough to study for exams.

Decide if you agree with any of these statements. Report back to the class.

Now, write a letter to your GCSE examining group giving your opinion on whether boys and girls should study more women's poetry for examinations. Follow these stages for success.

Step 1
Write a formal letter. Include your address, the date and the address of the examining group (your teacher will know this). Write to The Secretary.

Step 2
Make use of the opinions you have discussed in the first part of this activity to organise your writing into paragraphs.

Step 3
Choose three or four of the poems you have studied in this unit. Discuss them in detail as evidence for your opinions.

Step 4
Explain what GCSE English students will learn about women's issues and about how poetry works from studying women's poetry.

Step 5
Recommend two or three poets whose writing could be studied in depth for English Literature GCSE – and explain why you think they are suitable.

on target

After working through this unit, could you:

- write a poem of your own about your experience of growing up?

- explain to someone your own age how poetic techniques help a poem communicate its meaning?

- discuss the issues raised in other poems written by women?

Reading non-fiction

Travellers' tales

Travel writing tells of a time the writer spent away from home,
usually – but not always – in a strange and unfamiliar place. Some
travel writing is similar to diary writing and autobiography,
because travellers sometimes record the details of each day of a
voyage and often write in the first person.

**In this unit you will read and discuss four examples of
travel writing. You will role play an interview with a
traveller and write a traveller's tale of your own.**

Reading
about journeys

> Copy the chart below. Read the four extracts on pages 70–77 and collect information about them on the chart.

Text	A	B	C	D
Year of journey				
Traveller's name				
Place described				
Mode of transport				
Problems encountered				
Memorable events				
Memorable people				
Style of writing – formal/colloquial				
Effect on reader – excitement/humour				
Purpose of writing – describing/making a point				

Text A   Arriving

Inspired by Jules Vernes' famous story *Around the World in Eighty Days*, Nick Sanders set off on his bicycle on a similar journey. Here he describes how he took the plane to Bombay.

It was *Day 25* and the flight to Santa Cruz airport in Bombay took me into the early morning of *Day 26*. At least for the duration of the flight, I could rest in relative comfort. I liked flying.

Normally I sleep when flying but sitting next to me was a man from England.

'I'm a community worker from Manchester,' he said introducing himself, 'I've been planning this trip for three years and it's been in my head for ten years.' Peter had a kind warm face with wrinkles around eyes that allowed for lots of smiling. He also had raised eyebrows, a characteristic I associated with listening. 'I've been in Turkey these past two months. It's a great place. If you ever go, try and get to the underground city around Capadocia.' 'I've spent three days in Turkey,' I told him, 'and saw nothing but the open road.'

He raised his eyebrows, listening in disbelief. As he smoked a cigarette, he looked at me apprehensively. 'Do you think India will live up to my dreams? Is it really full of poor people and lepers?' 'It's a beautiful country, the people are friendly in a way that doesn't exist in the West.' I paused before giving him a gentle warning. 'Do be careful. What is only a day's spending money to you is a week's wages to some people. In the wrong place at the wrong time you could be killed.'

I, too, was concerned about the Indian section of the journey. The sheer enormity of the country with her 700 million people is part of the experience. My apprehension was composed of love and loathing: to love the feeling of excitement, adventuring in foreign lands, and to loathe the inevitable feeling of a stomach clogged up with 'butterflies'.

'Waiting in the departure lounge I was with a girl who was so nervous she could hardly hold her cigarette.' He pointed her out to me and I turned around to look at her. Her lips were quivering and when she saw me, she gave me a frightened smile. 'I got this letter from me Mum,' Peter continued, 'a thousand words it was, asking me why I don't settle down and stop this larking about.' He paused for a second, 'I wrote back suggesting her life was boring and tedious with a husband she hasn't spoken to properly for thirty years.' 'I've been trying to tell the kids on television that they could bike around the world if they wanted to,' I said, 'but I may have underestimated the difficulties.' 'I showed my Indian visa to an Indian lad in Brixton,' he added, 'and he didn't even know where India was, so what's the point in saying he could bike round the world?' For a moment I was silent. I felt so sick I couldn't speak. 'What's the matter?' he asked, 'you've gone white.' 'I haven't got a visa.' I said, only too aware of the dreadful implications for my journey.

When the British colonised India, visas were not required. After Independence in 1947, any British passport holder could reside there unconditionally for 49 years.

'It's the Sikhs,' he said, 'they've been relying on their British passport to get in and cause trouble, new legislation, very recent.' What happened in Jordan could happen all over again. This was crazy. I thought that I had prepared for this trip so well. It was Robbie Burns who said, 'the best laid plans of mice and men aft gang agley,' and he was so right.

'They could lug you back to Cairo,' Peter said helpfully, brushing his stubbly chin. 'A friend of mine hadn't got a visa and they locked him up for five days until they got it all sorted out.'

Nick Sanders (from *The Great Bike Ride*)

Text B   Travelling by river

At the end of the nineteenth century, Mary Kingsley wrote about her travels in Africa. Like many Victorian explorers, she was interested in collecting plants and insects unknown to Europeans. Her journeys sometimes led her into danger, as this description of the rapids of the Ogowé River shows.

Now and again we ran up against great rocks sticking up in the black water – grim, isolated fellows, who seemed to be standing silently watching their fellow rocks noisily fighting in the arena of the white water. Still on we poled and paddled. About 8 pm we came to a corner, a bad one. We fought our way round that corner, yelling defiance at the water, and dealt with succeeding corners on the *vi et armis* plan, breaking ever and anon, a pole. About 8.30 we got into a savage rapid. We fought it inch by inch. The canoe jammed herself on some barely sunken rocks in it. We shoved her off over them. She tilted over and chucked us out. The rocks round being just awash, we survived and got her straight again, and got into her and drove her unmercifully; she struck again and bucked like a broncho, and we fell in heaps upon each other but stayed inside that time – the men by the aid of their intelligent feet, I by clinching my hands into the bush rope lacing which ran round the rim of the canoe and the meaning of which I did not understand when I left Talagouga. We sorted ourselves out hastily and sent her at it again. Smash went a sorely tried pole and a paddle. Round and round we spun in an exultant whirlpool, which, in a light-hearted, maliciously joking way, hurled us tail first out of it into the current. Now the grand point in these canoes of having both ends alike declared itself; for at this juncture all we had to do was to revolve on our own axis and commence life anew with what had been the bow for the stern. Of course we were defeated, we could not go up any further without the aid of our lost poles and paddles, so we had to go down for shelter somewhere, anywhere, and down at a terrific pace in the white water we

went. While hitched among the rocks the arrangement of our crew had been altered, Pierre joining M'bo in the bows; this piece of precaution was frustrated by our getting turned round; so our position was what you might call precarious, until we got into another whirlpool, when we persuaded nature to start us right end on. This was only a matter of minutes, whirlpools being plentiful, and then M'bo and Pierre, provided with our surviving poles, stood in the bows to fend us off rocks, as we

shot towards them; while we midship paddles sat, helping to steer, and when occasion arose, which occasion did with lightning rapidity, to whack the whirlpools with the flat of our paddles, to break their force. Cook crouched in the stern concentrating his mind on steering only. A most excellent arrangement in theory and the safest practical one no doubt, but it did not work out what you might call brilliantly well; though each department did its best. We dashed full tilt towards high rocks, things twenty to fifty feet above water. Midship backed and flapped like fury; M'bo and Pierre received the shock on their poles; sometimes we glanced successfully aside and flew on; sometimes we didn't. The shock being too much for M'bo and Pierre they were driven back on me, who got flattened on to the cargo of bundles which, being now firmly tied in, couldn't spread the confusion further aft; but the shock of the canoe's nose against the rock did so in style, and the rest of the crew fell forward on to the bundles, me, and themselves. So shaken up together were we several times that night, that it's a wonder to me, considering the hurry, that we sorted ourselves correctly with our own particular legs and arms. And although we in the middle of the canoe did some very spirited flapping, our whirlpool-breaking was no more successful than M'bo and Pierre's fending off, and many a wild waltz we danced that night with the waters of the River Ogowé.

Unpleasant as going through the rapids was, when circumstances took us into the black current we fared no better. For good all round inconvenience, give me going full tilt in the dark into the branches of a fallen tree at the pace we were going then – and crash, swish, crackle and there you are, hung up, with a bough pressing against your chest, and your hair being torn out and your clothes ribboned by others, while the wide river is trying to draw away the canoe from under you. I expect we should have been an amusing spectacle for hard-hearted onlookers; but onlookers there were none, neither could we form a cooperative society for consuming our own ridiculousness as we did when we had light to see it by. After a good hour and more of these experiences, we went hard on to a large black reef of rocks. So firm was the canoe wedged that we in our rather worn out state couldn't move her so we wisely decided to 'lef 'em' and see what could be done towards getting food and a fire for the remainder of the night.

Mary Kingsley (from Travels in West Africa)

Text C   Travelling on foot

Travel writing does not have to be about expensive journeys to faraway places. In this extract, Mark Wallington writes about walking around the coast of Cornwall with a dog called Boogie.

Three weeks out, and a diurnal pattern was beginning to emerge. I wake and get moving at three thirty each morning, stopping for breakfast when it was warmed up. During the morning we'd walk about ten miles until midday when we'd stop in some suitable town or village and frequently embarrass ourselves with the amount we'd eat. Whole loaves and lettuces and boxes of Winalot would disappear, accompanied by pasties and slabs of cheese, tomatoes, apples, chocolate and pints of milk.

After that we'd stop for lunch and then relax during the afternoon with a variety of activities. Boogie's favourites were seeing how long he could stare at the sun without going blind, or else chasing flies. Me, I was beginning to take a healthy interest in rubbish.

I've always enjoyed beachcombing. You never know what you're going to find: a lump of the Armada one day, a bit of orange peel the next. Most of what I was finding on these shores, however, was plastic bottles.

I'd noticed litter along the strandline throughout Cornwall and just assumed it to be the usual picnickers' debris. But picnickers don't bring bottles of shampoo and washing-up liquid down to the beach with them; at least they don't bring Russian or Spanish brands, but that's what these were: pieces of international rubbish, obviously thrown overboard from ships steaming along this marine motorway. I quickly learnt the Polish for Head and Shoulders, and experienced the thrill of finding my first bottle of Brazilian disinfectant.

We'd begin walking again in the late afternoon, buying food in the last village of the day, then keep going into the evening; they were growing longer and warmer now and were good times to walk, and we'd not camp until the sun had but an hour left in the sky.

The day we passed through Falmouth, that last village was Portloe. Charming, I noted in my diary later, noting also that, as had happened with the sky, the search for adjectives to suitably describe fishing villages was putting a strain on my vocabulary; delightful, cute, enchanting, idyllic, picturesque, exquisite, nice, I'd used them all.

I walked up the main street and quickly found the post office stores. I was tired and I was weathered, but above all I was hungry.

'Can of mushroom soup and a can of Kennomeat, please,' I said to the lady behind the grille. She clasped her hands and shook her head. I scanned the shelves behind her. If I'd wanted a TV licence I'd have been all right, but soup and Kennomeat, in fact sustenance of any sort, was right out.

'But I was told you sold provisions here,' I said; the thought of another night on limpets and nettles injecting a hint of desperation into my tone.

Again she clasped her hands and shook her head. I decided on a more hysterical approach. 'But, but, but, look at my poor dog, he's been walking all day and he's starving.' Her face crumpled as Boogie laid his head on the counter and, sensing the gravity of the situation, drew from his vast wardrobe of expressions the 'been walking all day and now starving' mask.

Then the woman had a brainwave. She'd phone her sister who kept a small store in Port Holland, the next village along the coast. She'd stay open for me until six, she said. It was two miles. I had half an hour. It was going to be close.

If Heinrich Harrer* had found himself in a similar situation, there'd have been none of this panic, of course. He'd simply have eaten his dog. As I strode along the cliffs, I tried to banish the thought. I mean, what could I tell Sean – I ate his dog because the post office was shut. Hardly gallant. It wasn't as if Boogie was a particularly tasty looking dish, anyway. He was stringy, probably tough and sinewy, all dark meat, the kind of dog Amundsen** would have left on the side of his plate. Mind you, he might taste better if I barbecued him, put him on a spit over a driftwood fire. Hadn't I seen a Chinese recipe for cooking dogs, recently? 'How to Wok your Pekinese,' or something.

I wondered if he'd put up a fight. I mean, how would I do the dastardly deed? Push him off a cliff; maybe just club him, or stab him with a tent pole; better still, run one through him, then he'd be all ready to go on the spit. It wasn't that I didn't appreciate the sacrifice, but there was no room for sentimentality. This was the ultimate altruistic act for a dog, and I should make sure I made the most of the gesture. I'd try and make him last over a few days. Eat him leg by leg, in a goulash on Wednesday, curry on Thursday, dog supreme on Friday, and in sandwiches or cold with cranberry sauce and salad over the weekend when I didn't want to have to cook. I was contemplating a bowl of thin but nourishing dog soup when Port Holland came into view: a row of cottages, a telephone kiosk and the stores.

The sister was waiting for us. She stroked Boogie affectionately, told him he needn't have worried, she wouldn't have let him go hungry, then offered him a choice of Pal, Chappie or Lassie Meaty Chunks. She checked he had enough milk and biscuit for the morning and before she closed up she even sold me a can of soup.

Mark Wallington (from 500 Miles Walkies)

* Heinrich Harrer – German soldier who escaped from British prisoner-of-war camp in Nepal and took refuge in Tibet, an experience he later described in his book, *Seven Years in Tibet*.

** Amundsen – Norwegian explorer who reached the South Pole in 1911, a month before Captain Scott.

Text D   Reaching a destination

Maya Angelou, the black American writer, lived, worked and travelled in Ghana during the 1960s. This memorable description of her experiences in the small town of Keta, in Eastern Ghana, comes towards the end of her autobiographical account of her stay in Africa.

The narrow stairs were bounded by wooden walls, making the entrance dim. I was looking down, making certain of my footfall, when a voice above me drew my attention. I looked up to see an older woman, unusually tall, blotting out the light behind her. She spoke again and in a voice somewhat similar to my own, but I was unable to understand her.

I smiled and, using Fanti, said regretfully, 'I am sorry, Auntie, but I don't speak Ewe.' She put her hands on her wide hips, reared back and let loose into the dim close air around us a tirade of angry words. When she stopped, I offered, in French and in a self-deprecating tone, 'I am sorry, Auntie, but I don't speak Ewe.'

She clapped her hands close enough to my face for me to feel the rush of air, then she raised her voice. My ignorance of the meaning of her words did not prevent me from knowing that I was being denounced in the strongest possible language.

When I could wedge myself into her explosion, I spoke in English nearly whining, 'Auntie, I am sorry, but I do not speak Ewe.'

Mr Adadevo stepped up and placed himself between me and my assailant. He spoke softly in Ewe. I heard the word 'American' while I was watching the woman's face. She shook her head in denial. My protector spoke again, still softly. I heard 'American Negro'. Still the woman's face showed disbelief.

Mr Adadevo looked at me and said 'Sister, she thinks you're someone else. Do you have your American passport with you?'

I hadn't seen my passport in two years, but I remembered having an old California driver's license, which had its identifying photograph. I took the wrinkled, but still slick paper from my wallet and gave it to Mr Adadevo. He handed the document to the woman who strained to see in the darkness. She turned and walked up the stairs into the light.

Mr Adadevo followed and I followed him.

There, the woman, who was over six feet tall, stood peering at the flimsy piece of paper in her dark hand. When she raised her head, I nearly fell back down the steps; she had the wide face and slanted eyes of my grandmother. Her lips were large and beautifully shaped like my grandmother's and her cheek bones were high like those of my grandmother. The woman solemnly returned the license to Mr Adadevo who gave it back to me, then the woman reached out and touched my shoulder hesitantly. She softly patted my cheek a few times. Her face had changed. Outrage had given way to melancholia. After a few seconds of studying me, the woman lifted both arms and lacing her fingers together clasped her hands and put them on the top of her head. She rocked a little from side to side and issued a pitiful little moan.

In Arkansas, when I was a child, if my brother or I put our hands on our heads as the woman before me was doing, my grandmother would stop in her work and come to remove our hands and warn us that the gesture brought bad luck.

Mr Adadevo spoke to me quietly, 'That's the way we mourn.'

My guide now pulled me through a press of bodies until we came to a stall where the owner sold yams, cassava and other tubers. Her wares were stacked on the ground in front of the stall and rose in piles

around the stool she occupied. My escort began her litany to the saleswoman. Somewhere in the ritual she said 'American Negro' and the woman repeated the first stall owner's behaviour. Freida began putting yams and cocoa yams and cassava into her basket. The two women were rocking and moaning. I said,

'Mr Adadevo, you must tell me what's happening.'

He said, 'This is a very sad story and I can't tell it all or tell it well.' I waited while he looked around. He began again. 'During the slavery period Keta was a good sized village. It was hit very hard by the slave trade. Very hard. In fact, at one point every inhabitant was either killed or taken. The only escapees were children who ran away and hid in the bush. Many of them watched from their hiding places as their parents were beaten and put into chains. They saw the slaves set fire to the village. They saw mothers and fathers take infants by their feet and bash their heads against tree trunks rather than see them sold into slavery. What they saw they remembered and all that they remembered they told over and over.

'The children were taken in by nearby villagers and grew to maturity. They married and had children and rebuilt Keta. They told the tale to their offspring. These women are the descendants of those orphaned children. They have heard the stories often, and the deeds are still as fresh as if they happened during their lifetimes. And you, Sister, you look so much like them, even the tone of your voice is like theirs. They are sure you are descended from those stolen mothers and fathers. That is why they mourn. Not for you but for their lost people.'

A sadness descended on me, simultaneously sombre and wonderful. I had not consciously come to Ghana to find the roots of my beginnings, but I had continually and accidentally tripped over them or fallen upon them in my everyday life.

Maya Angelou (from All God's Children Need Travelling Shoes)

Language in use

FORMAL AND COLLOQUIAL STYLES

The style of a piece of writing is related to its purpose and audience. Formal writing is writing for a public, unknown audience, where the material is largely factual and made up of information. An informal, or colloquial, style is for writing where the audience is more familiar and the material mixes facts and opinions. Travel writing provides examples of both styles:

Named after its designer, Gustave Eiffel, the Eiffel Tower is 320 metres high but this figure can vary by up to 15cm as the 2.5 million rivets that hold it together expand in warm weather and contract in cold. The tower is open daily from 9.30 am to 11 pm.

Fight your way through the crowds to the stairs in the south pillar, pay 10FF, take a deep breath and climb what seems like a million stairs to the second platform which is almost half way. The crowds push, the staircases smell, but the view from the top is fantastic.

The main difference between these two descriptions is the sense of audience and the vocabulary used. The formal writing is full of information about the tower, presented in a factual way. However, the informal writing addresses the reader as 'you' and assumes that you are young enough to take what is quite a steep climb. The writing exaggerates, or is deliberately not quite accurate – 'a million stairs', 'half way up' – and full of opinions – 'the staircases smell' – as well as facts.

5

2 Interview a traveller

Working in pairs, role play an interview that takes place on a television chat show with one of the travellers. Follow these steps for success.

Step 1

Decide which one of you will be the interviewer. The other will be one of the four travellers promoting the book of his or her journey.

Step 2

Using your chart to help you, make up ten questions the interviewer can ask the traveller.

Talk, and make notes, about the replies the traveller is likely to give. These should be based on the information in the text, but you will need to think about how the traveller would communicate those replies. Would he or she try to amuse the audience, convey a sense of danger or try to describe somewhere unusual as accurately as possible?

Step 3

Practise your interview. The interviewer should try to steer the conversation towards interesting events and ask questions that follow on from what the traveller says. The traveller should remember that the more interesting he or she can make his or her book sound, the more copies it will sell!

... on interviews based on reading

 The interviewer should:

- re-read the text carefully
- avoid closed questions that can be answered 'yes' or 'no'
- ask open questions which begin with words like 'How?', 'Why?' and 'What happened when ... ?'
- make sure that the interview begins and ends smoothly
- listen to what the traveller says and ask follow-up questions
- show interest in what the traveller says, perhaps by nodding and smiling.

 The traveller should:

- make sure his or her answers reflect the text accurately
- try not to repeat the extract exactly but concentrate on the events and feelings described and think about how to express them in speech
- make eye contact with the interviewer and the audience
- show excitement or amusement through gesture and expression
- try to look relaxed and confident.

Write about a journey

Travel writing can be based on familiar scenes looked at in a new or interesting way.

> Write a magazine article about a time when you made a memorable journey. The journey does not have to be to somewhere exotic: it could be as simple as a walk or a bus ride around an area you do not visit regularly. Follow these steps to success.

Step 1
Think about your writing as a whole

Decide on your journey
Do not feel you have to describe the whole trip from beginning to end – a more detailed description of one incident may be better.

Decide on the way you are going to write
Will your style be serious or amusing, formal or informal?

Decide on your audience
What sort of magazine are you writing for? Is your writing aimed at adults or children?

Decide on your purpose
Do you want your writing to excite or frighten your readers? Do you want to inspire them to follow in your footsteps or to share your feelings about the beauty of a place?

Step 2
Plan what you intend to write

Make a plan or notes
Note down people, places, events you may include.

Decide on a beginning and end
Remember that your opening paragraph will determine whether the reader keeps reading to the end of your article.

Give your writing a title
Make sure that the title reflects your purpose.

Step 3
Draft, revise and proof-read
Keep the final version for your coursework portfolio.

on target

After working through this unit, could you:

- describe some of the distinctive features of travel writing?

- recognise the main purpose of another piece of travel writing?

- keep a travel journal on the next journey you make?

Within the photograph, the following job vacancy notices are visible:

KEEPINTOUCH

FARRINGDON RECORDS

VACANCY SENIOR POLICY ADVISER
DISTRICT: CENTRAL LONDON
WAGE: £25,321 - £27,502
HOURS: T.B.A.
DETAILS: LEAD A TEAM - PROVIDE
ADVICE ON SPECIAL NEEDS
HOUSING + HOUSING FOR OLDER
PEOPLE - 5 YEARS RELEVANT EXP
- 2 YEARS AT MANAGERIAL LEVEL
ASK FOR HJC 891

VACANCY SHOP MANAGER
DISTRICT: BOND STREET
WAGE: £12,000
HOURS: SHOP HOURS / FLEXIBLE
DETAILS: PREV. EXP. AS MANAGER
+ INTEREST IN CERAMICS -
ANOTHER LANGUAGE AN ASSET
- GOOD REFS. REQUIRED
ASK FOR WND 1166

JOBCENTRESHE

Reading non-literary material

Qualified for work

During the 1990s, more people will gain more qualifications than ever before. Most sixteen year olds already stay on at school, or go to college, to gain further qualifications. But adults who left school without taking examinations are now joining their children in the classroom in order to improve their own career opportunities.

In this unit you will practise different ways of reading as you find out information about qualifications and work. You will write an assignment that brings together ideas and information from the extracts you have read.

Reading for overall impression

Often you want to read something to find out what it is about without going into details. This is called *skimming*.

Skim read the texts which follow to gain an idea of what they are about. Make a copy of the chart on page 87 and work in pairs to complete the details.

Text A

This is the opening of a full-length cartoon story for adults, written by Raymond Briggs.

Page 1

Page 2

Page 3

Raymond Briggs (from Gentleman Jim)

Text B

This is a chapter from the middle of an autobiography telling of the childhood and early adulthood of Joyce Storey. It was written when she became involved in a community writing project in her home town, Bristol.

My first job

It was a day like any other day when I walked for the last time out of the playground of Two Mile Hill Girls' School in 1931. No friends milled around me to wish me luck as I now ventured into the frightening world of adult life. My fourteenth birthday had coincided with the end of term holidays.

Everybody was eager for the six weeks break. Six of us had been handed a long brown envelope and, once outside, I ripped it open to read my mind-shattering school testimonial. This precious slip of paper would go with me on every job I ever wrote or answered an advertisement for. I glanced down at Miss Duggan's sprawling handwriting; on a twelve-inch square piece of vellum paper it stated simply:

'This is to certify that Beryl Joyce Dark has been a pupil of this school for the past seven years. Having reached the accepted standard her general work is good. Her regularity is good. Her conduct is good. She is clean and neat in appearance. She is honest and truthful.'

Not much, I thought bitterly, to be armed with out there in that big world and the great workforce that I was about to become part of. I guessed that the ability to rise and shine at some unearthly hour and to be able to clock in on the dot was far more important than any academic qualification.

Before coming out into the freedom and sunshine, I had taken one last look around the hall. I noted the Honours Boards with the names of girls who had won scholarships, their names emblazoned for all to

see in letters of gold. From the whole school perhaps only one would be fortunate to gain the coveted place, and for a whole year she would be placed on a pedestal as a shining example of what we could all achieve through the gracious auspices of our wonderful educational system which was the best in the world.

I had made no such mark of distinction. Little Miss Average I, along with a million other Miss Averages. No one would ever know that we had ever been inside those walls. Miss Duggan's desk stood on a raised wooden platform in the recess by the window, enforcing the impression that this was the 'Head' and let everybody bend the knee. The very name commanded respect. The cane, symbol of discipline, hung in front of the desk for all to see and mark well. the Punishment and Reward system never failed. You behaved yourself, or else. I often felt the swish of the cane hurtling down on my defenceless palm. The sting came later when my palm smarted for hours along with dark thoughts that never quite eradicated the fear.

I stopped only once more at the forge at the top of the lane where old Tom Pillinger was making the sparks fly and I listened to the chink of hammer on steel as he shoed a horse. Now no more would I stand fascinated and silent as the horse stood patiently waiting for her new shoes. The stopping and the running on to the school was part of a very intimate school scene; it was as important as the four red Indian eyes you got at the tuck shop for a ha'penny. I felt tearful and sad, tossed about with emotions I didn't understand and couldn't cope with. At fourteen I didn't feel grown up and, what was more, I didn't want to.

Joyce Storey (from Our Joyce)

Text C

This poem was one of the winners of a competition for pupils at school in London.

You never took me

I have six CSEs to be exact
I knew you wouldn't take me
and that's a fact.

When I had 'phoned for the job
I spoke very well
Though I was black
you just couldn't tell.

I went for the job
looking my best
I even passed your typing test.

When I had arrived for the job
I saw your surprise
and then you filled me
with all of your lies.

You said to me you
wanted someone older.
A lump in my throat
I shrugged my shoulder.

You said 'I'll hope you understand.'
Then I arose and you shook my hand.

Yes; your reason I do understand!
You never took me and that's a fact.
You never took me because I'm Black.

Engley Stewart

Text D

This is an extract from a recent article published in the *Times Educational Supplement* – a weekly newspaper for teachers.

Adult student boom on the way

A massive upsurge in numbers of adult returners demanding degree courses is being predicted by further education colleges.

The explosion in demand expected in two to three years will create a tremendous squeeze on places.

Colleges are astonished at an upsurge in demand for places on access courses which pave the way for people without traditional qualifications to go to university. Some have seen steady growth over the decade, but most report very big increases in demand of around 50 per cent – suggesting that universities will see a similar increase in applications in a couple of years.

Principals believe the disappearance of low-skill jobs mean people are beginning to recognise the need to gain higher qualifications in an increasingly competitive market.

Tony Higgins, chief executive of the Universities and Colleges Admissions Service, said: 'If this is true then this must be good news. But where is the money to come from for the expansion?

'This year school-leavers and adults are saying to us: "We cannot afford to become students". If expectations are created, then HE has to be funded properly.'

A Department for Education report next week is expected to confirm that for the first time more adults entered university last year than 18-year-old school-leavers. The trend looks set to continue.

Predictions of high recruitment to General National Vocational Qualification courses, or vocational A levels, are borne out, although many colleges said science was struggling. Numbers on adult education courses are up on last year.

Ian Nash and *Neil Hutton*

(from the *Times Educational Supplement*, 26 September 1994)

Text E

These facts and figures come from a pamphlet produced by The National Advisory Council for Education and Training Targets, a committee set up by the government to try to improve the level of qualifications of working people in Britain.

National targets for education and training

Foundation Learning

Foundation Target 1

By 1997, 80% of young people to reach NVQ 2 or 5 GCSEs at grades A-C

In 1994, 63.4% of young people, up to and including age 19, have achieved either 5 GCSEs at grades A-C, an NVQ/SVQ 2 or vocational equivalent.

Foundation Target 2

Training and education to NVQ 3 or 2 A levels available to all young people who can benefit

Foundation Target 3

By 2000, 50% of young people to reach NVQ 3 or 2 A levels

In 1994, 41.5% of young people, up to and including age 21, have achieved 2 A levels, an NVQ/SVQ 3 or vocational equivalent.

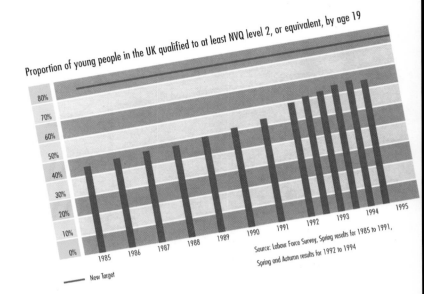

Proportion of young people in the UK qualified to at least NVQ level 2, or equivalent, by age 19

Source: Labour Force Survey, Spring results for 1985 to 1991, Spring and Autumn results for 1992 to 1994

—— New Target

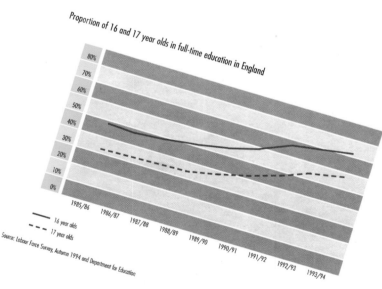

Proportion of 16 and 17 year olds in full-time education in England

—— 16 year olds
- - - 17 year olds

Source: Labour Force Survey, Autumn 1994 and Department for Education

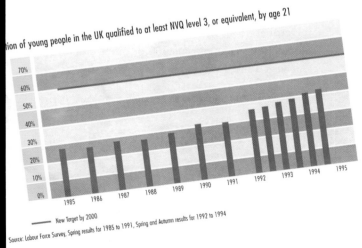

...tion of young people in the UK qualified to at least NVQ level 3, or equivalent, by age 21

—— New Target by 2000

Source: Labour Force Survey, Spring results for 1985 to 1991, Spring and Autumn results for 1992 to 1994

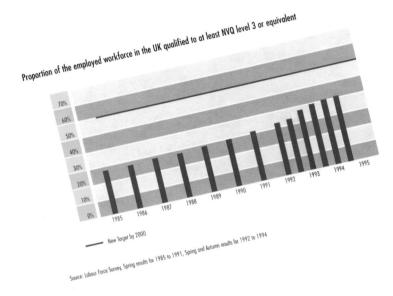

Proportion of the employed workforce in the UK qualified to at least NVQ level 3 or equivalent

—— New Target by 2000

Source: Labour Force Survey, Spring results for 1985 to 1991, Spring and Autumn results for 1992 to 1994

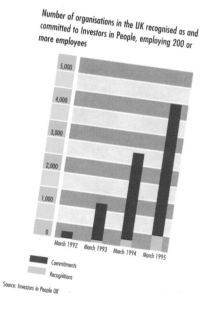

Number of organisations in the UK recognised as and committed to Investors in People, employing 200 or more employees

■ Commitments
▨ Recognitions

Source: Investors in People UK

Lifetime Learning
Lifetime Target 3

By 2000, 50% of the workforce qualified to at least NVQ 3 or 2 A levels

In 1994, 40.5% of the workforce possess either 2 A levels, an NVQ/SVQ 3, its vocational equivalent or higher level qualification.

Lifetime Target 4

By 1996, 50% of medium to larger organisations to be Investors in People

The first Investors in People were announced in October 1991. By the end of March 1995, 514 organisations employing 200 or more employees had achieved the Investors in People award.

The National Advisory Council for Education and Training Targets

Title: what is it called?	Author: who wrote it?	Type of text: what would you call this type of writing?	Purpose: why was it written?	Gist: what is it about?	Approximate date: when was it written?
A		Cartoon strip			
B					1930s
C					
D			To give information		
E		Figures and graph			1995

... on reading strategies

 Skimming
Skimming means reading quickly to gain a general idea of the types of text you have been given and getting the gist of what they are about.

 Scanning
Scanning means reading to look for particular information – reading quickly to find the relevant part of a text, then reading that part more carefully.

 Close reading
Close reading means paying attention to every word: thinking about the ideas expressed between the lines and also the writer's choice of language.

2 Reading for information

Now, scan the texts to collect information. Answer the questions below and make a note of the text you used and what the writer has to say about it. Organise your information on a chart like the one below.

a   Why do adults sometimes choose to take the same courses as school-leavers – like GCSEs and A Levels?

b   What percentage of sixteen year olds stayed on at school in 1986 and 1994?

c   What was the school-leaving age in 1931?

d   What is an 'access' course? Why do people take this kind of course?

e   What qualifications do you need to become an Officer in the Marines?

f   What percentage of people of working age are expected to have either 2 A Levels or NVQ level 3 qualifications by the year 2000?

g   What evidence can you find that unskilled jobs are disappearing, or are now often done by machines?

h   How has the way schools prepare school-leavers for work changed over the last 60 years?

Question	Text used	Information/opinion given by the writer
a		

3 Practise close reading

Some of these texts put forward opinions and ideas as well as giving you information. To understand these fully you need to do some detailed reading. (The Tips box opposite gives some suggestions for doing this.)

Work with a partner. Each choose a different text. Write five questions that focus on the main ideas or opinions of the text.

Exchange your work with your partner and try to answer his or her questions. Look at the texts you have worked on and discuss how this activity has helped you get a clearer idea of their meaning.

... on close reading

1 Using a pencil, make a copy of the text and annotate it to record things you noticed and thought about as you read. Here is a poem that has been annotated in this way:

Work is not really connected with her studies – on the surface

Cleaning under this bed is
the married woman sociology student
who is working all through her vacations
as she doesn't get a grant
(her husband works all through his vacations
as a porter
and gets 30% more)
She has noticed with excitement
how nobody looks at cleaning women
or respects them *
Nobody looks at students pretending
to be cleaning women either
(they don't join unions)
Everyone notices her accent
She talks loudly because her husband never listens
'Aren't you rather educated to be a cleaner, cleaner?'
they ask her constantly.
'Oh, you're a student.'
She's going to put it all in her dissertation.
She can't imagine how people who
work there always
put up with it
She gave in her notice today, gratefully
after ten weeks

Diana Scott

adult student

working to pay for her studies

BUT

her experience as a cleaner gives her ideas for her studies

gender discrimination??? why does a porter earn more than a cleaner?

no means of complaining about the work or the low pay no name!

She speaks in a more educated manner than the others

She doesn't enjoy the work – though it has given her some ideas for her sociology course

*sounds as if she gets ignored at home as well as at work

Lots of negative words – doesn't, nobody, don't, can't, etc – reflects her negative feelings??

2 Ask yourself questions about the meaning of words or sentences which are difficult, or which seem to have some kind of hidden message. For this extract from a poem, useful questions might be:

- Why does the poet tell us that the cleaner is studying sociology?

- What do we learn about the cleaner's husband? What does this tell us about their relationship?

- What do other people in the hospital think about the cleaners?

- What is the student's opinion of the job and the cleaners she works with?

- How does she see herself as different from them?

Language in use

THE VISUAL MEDIA

'The media' is a term that covers all the forms of mass communication in our society. This includes:

- the *publishing* of books, magazines and newspapers in printed forms;
- the *production* of films, videos and music;
- the *creation* of advertisements, images and illustrations;
- and *broadcasting* from radio, television and satellite.

The definition of the media is always changing. Electronic publishing, the world of virtual reality and the development of computerised communications are some of the most recent developments that are now said to form part of the media.

Although 'media texts' (the products of the media) have many similarities with written texts, they also differ significantly. For this reason, it helps to have a different set of questions to ask about such texts. Here are six such questions (you could compare them with the questions on page 88):

What sort of product is it?	CATEGORY	Identifying different types of product (documentary, soap opera, etc: fact and fiction, and different media (cinema, press, etc): thinking about how different categories influence expectations and understanding.
What does it mean?	LANGUAGE	Carefully looking at/listening to everything in a media product: thinking about how we interpret the media and how we can make a product (e.g. video, photo) say what we mean: learning how to understand e.g. close-up, fade-out, etc: understanding and using sequences, story structures, etc.
Who made it?	AGENCY	Learning about who makes media products and why: what they cost, how long they take to make, etc: different jobs in the production process.
How was it made?	TECHNOLOGY	Finding out what kinds of technology are available and to whom: how to use them: the difference that a choice of technology makes to how something is made and what it looks/sounds like.
Who is it for?	AUDIENCE	Discovering that an audience can be people you don't know: how audiences can be reached: how audiences get to see/hear media products: what their reactions are.
What is the message?	REPRESENTATION	Thinking about the relationship between a media product and reality: making judgements about, and comparing, products that are meant to be realistic (e.g. news, war films) with ones that aren't (e.g. cartoons, horror films): what makes something frightening, shocking, stereotyped, exaggerated, implausible, authentic, etc.

© BFI Education Department

6

Use your reading

Imagine that you have been asked to provide some information for an educational television programme, aimed at GCSE students, to be called *Qualified for Work*. The programme is intended to emphasise the increasing importance of education in preparing people of all ages for the job market.

Write a formal letter to the producer of the programme, Corinne Dunnant. Suggest to her that she uses three of the texts you have read in this unit as part of the programme. Her address is:

> National Gold Productions
> Docklands House
> Reith Road
> London SE3 5TV

In your letter, describe each of the texts you have selected, say what information they contain and suggest how they could be adapted or portrayed on television to have most impact.

... on adapting texts

Organise your letter into paragraphs by explaining the points you think the programme should make and how your chosen extracts will help communicate these ideas. As you work:

- avoid simply summarising each of your chosen texts in turn;
- think about how the extracts could be presented on television;
- end by offering any further help or advice which may be necessary.

The extracts could be used in different ways, for example:

- shown on the screen;
- read aloud by actors;
- dramatised;
- used as voice-overs while still photographs are shown.

on target

After working through this unit, could you:

- explain to another GCSE student how to use different reading strategies to find information from different texts about a topic?

- apply close reading techniques you have learned to other poems or stories?

- select the best texts to use for an assignment, when you are provided with a large number to choose from?

Reading the media

The home of the future

Science has changed our lives dramatically in the last hundred years. People born at the start of this century may have seen the first aeroplanes: now they watch news of the latest space shuttles on their colour television. Within the last few decades, the room-sized computers used by big businesses have been replaced by cheap, portable computers that fit into a briefcase.

In this unit you will discuss the effects of inventions on our everyday lives and consider what developments the future may hold. You will talk and write about the pace of technological change and how consumers are persuaded to buy new products.

Look at change

On a large sheet of paper, list all the twentieth-century inventions you can think of in five minutes (this is called a brainstorm). To help you get started, think about the worlds of transport, communications, medicine and entertainment.

Select *five* inventions from your list which you think have most changed the way people live. Then, discuss each one in turn with a partner. As you talk, think about:

- whether the invention saves time, money or unpleasant work;
- how convenient it is;
- how many people's lives it has affected;
- whether it has been a success;
- whether it has been worthwhile.

Each group should now choose one invention and report the group's views back to the class.

Some opinions about modern inventions

'My daughter can't do her maths without a calculator. My generation is better at doing sums in their heads.'

'I don't know what I'd do if I didn't have my television. Now I'm not as mobile as I used to be it keeps me in touch.'

'These cash cards are all very well, but I used to like it when they had time to have a chat with you over the counter in the bank.'

'My daughter and son drive me mad with their computer. We bought it to help their education, but all they seem to want to do is play violent and noisy games.'

'I work long hours, so my family needs labour-saving kitchen equipment. We'd find it hard to cope without the washer, the dish-washer, the microwave and all the other things that make looking after a family quick and easy.'

'With my mobile phone, I can easily keep in touch with suppliers, and my customers can easily get hold of me.'

'With these cameras and micro-surgery our patients get better quicker.'

2 Look at the future

Read the article below. Then, use the chart on page 96 to make a list of the innovations in the home of the future and what their benefits and disadvantages might be.

House of the future

Experts predict that, by the year 2013, scientists will have invented a computer that is as powerful as the human brain.

The new machine will not only be able to do much more than ever before, but will also be much simpler to operate. The whole family will be able to control everything in the home, from the front door to the lights, by simply speaking commands to the computer.

Here are just some of the advances which will be reality in the homes of the twenty-first century:

Video shopping

Virtual reality goggles and gloves which allow people to interact with imaginary worlds are already taking the place of video games. But in ten years we may be wearing virtual reality glasses to go shopping.

Just put on the specs and a thin glove to link into your computer and you will be 'transported' to the superstore of your choice, where computer pictures will display the shelves as if you were really there.

To make your selection just reach out your gloved hand and 'touch' the packet you want. The computer will note all you buy and how much you spend. Technology developed for fighter pilots allows any special offers to be projected in front of you.

TV and video

The TV will be linked to satellite, cable and terrestrial channels rather like those of today but with a greater choice of programmes than ever before.

Thanks to computer techniques which compress many channels into the space one needs now, viewers could choose from 500 channels or more.

Television and computers will be integrated and work in the same, simple way. You can even be your own movie director thanks to interactive TV – which is already being developed. At certain points in a film, you can select from alternative story lines and create your own version. Or you can record bits of many programmes, add your own home movies, and edit them all together on your computer.

You won't even need to press a button to change channel or even know which station is showing your favourite programme. Ask the TV to find the news, for example, and clips of all news shows currently on air would appear on the screen for you to select from. Even the video will accept verbal instructions.

Front door

Juggling armfuls of carrier bags while fumbling for your keys will become a thing of, well, today.

The door locks will be connected to the household computer, which will automatically respond to your request to open the door. The computer will analyse your voice, verify it is you and let you in.

The system can also be programmed with a password where a pre-arranged phrase must be spoken to gain access to the house.

Home computer

Far removed from the computers of today, this will be the heart of the electronic home. Other equipment in the house will be controlled via it.

Dramatic advances in voice technology will do away with the electronic keyboard entirely.

If you want the living room lights dimmed, or the central heating temperature set, you will just tell the computer.

Answer machine

The answering machine will come of age and alert you to any important calls.

If you are away from the house you can programme the answering machine to ring your mobile phone at a pre-determined time and give you a list of all your callers.

You then tell it which of the calls you want to take and it will ring back those people for you.

The machine will also be linked to a database so it knows the numbers of your friends, relatives and business associates. This will allow the machine to screen your calls and only put through the ones you want to receive. The problem of teenagers running up huge phone bills will become a thing of the past. Every phone will be fitted with an electronic device to identify the person using it and, if necessary, end the call after a set time.

Home banking

You will be able to do everyday banking from your living room. All phones will be fitted with a small screen and a series of buttons. They will function just like a bank hole-in-the-wall machine.

Your phone will connect with the bank's computer. Once you are linked up, you will be able to order a cheque book, check the balance in your account and transfer money simply by pressing the buttons.

You will also be able to pay bills. Simply instruct the computer where to send the money and how much to pay.

If you want to speak to the bank manager just press another button and the computer will put you through to a human being.

Active wallpaper

By the year 2020 experts predict we will be able to watch TV on a screen the size of an entire wall in the home.

The secret is a material dubbed active wallpaper. Scientists can already produce liquid crystal displays which are paper-thin. After the turn of the century, we will be able to cover the walls of our homes in this material. Professor Peter Cochrane, who studies future technology, says: 'With active wallpaper you will never need to hang photographs again. You will be able to programme your computer to project ever changing 3-D images on to the wall.

'You could also use it to provide a moving mural or alter the colour of a room by using a voice command.'

Bathroom

Your home computer will know exactly how hot you like the water and how deep you would like it to be. Tell it 'Run me a bath at 10pm' and you will be able to step right into the water at 10pm on the dot.

Repairs

If your washing machine breaks down while you are at work, the home's computer will contact a plumber using the computer network. It will then call you about the problem and order the engineer to come round after you have given it the go-ahead.

The computer will let in the workman. If the engineer cannot cure the problem himself, he will put on a Camnet headset. The set has an inbuilt microphone and two tiny cameras, which are connected to an operator back at base. An engineer at the firm's headquarters will be able to see the problem for himself and instruct the workman on how to carry out the repair.

Kitchen

Your kitchen will be dominated by a large computer screen which obeys voice commands.

So you can order the electronic butler to switch on the cooker at whatever temperature you tell it.

Patrick Griffin (from *The Sun*, 12 August 1993)

Innovation	Advantages	Possible disadvantages

Compare the innovations you have read about. Select three which you think would improve people's lives and three which you consider pointless or possibly damaging.

Write about these six innovations, giving your reasons for selecting them.

Look at how the future is sold

How do advertisers persuade people to buy things they have previously managed without?

Study the advertisements on this page and the next. Make notes on how they try to persuade you to buy a product. Use the glossary on page 98 and the Tips box on page 99 to help you.

Pick one advertisement and write a short commentary on how successful it is. Use the headings in the Tips box to help you structure your writing. Follow these steps for success.

Step 1

Briefly say what the product is and describe what the advertisement shows.

Step 2

Write three or four paragraphs about what you see and read in the advertisement. Use the headings in the Tips box to help you get started. Make sure you write something about the use of illustration, the use of language and the target audience.

Step 3

Say how effective you think the advertisement will be in reaching its target audience. Give your reasons.

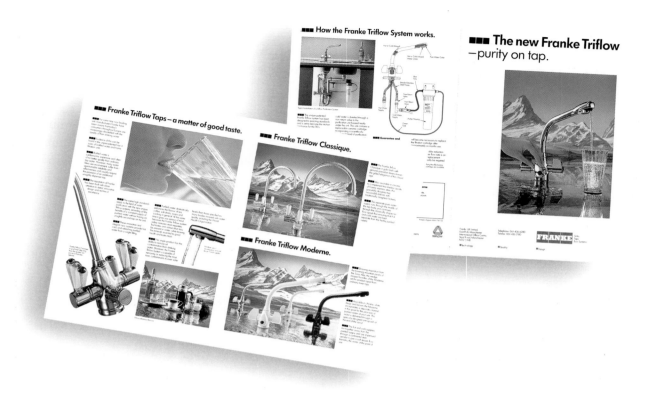

The language of advertising – glossary

product	the thing that the advertisers want to sell
copy	the text of an advertisement
target audience	the section of the population at which the advertisement is aimed
emotive words	the words or phrases that appeal to your feelings
images	the mix of illustrations (one picture or more) and words used to attract attention
slogan	the words or phrases that stand out – you notice them and they are easy to remember
persuasive language	the words that encourage you to react in a certain way by giving commands or asking questions
associations	what you think of, apart from the product, when you look at an advertisement
weasel words	the words that protect the advertiser against the charge of making untrue statements about the product – words like 'probably' and 'almost'
jargon	the use of scientific and technical words to impress the reader

... the top 20 questions to ask about advertisements

Look at the image

1   Does it show you the actual product, or does it show you something else?

2   Do the pictures create an image of modern living?

3   What associations do the pictures have? What message do they give about the product?

Look at the slogans

4   How does the advertisement catch your eye? A heading? A slogan? A brand name?

5   How are words and phrases positioned on the page?

6   How are headings used?

Look at the copy

7   What facts are you given about the product – statistics and technical terms?

8   Does the advertisement provide a list of features?

9   What is the product called? Is there a link between the name and the theme?

10   What does the advertisement tell you about the cost? What does it not tell you?

11   Where are you invited to change your opinion, or try something new?

Look at persuasive language

12   Are emotive words used?

13   Do adjectives praise the product, or knock the alternatives?

14   Does the advertisement use repetition to emphasise the selling point?

15   Does it use weasel words?

Look at register and style

16   Does the advertisement adopt the style of spoken language or try to be formal?

17   Where does it differ from normal written English? Do the sentences begin with connectives like 'then' and 'or', have no main verb or consist of only one word?

18   Are there questions, orders or occasions when the reader is addressed as 'you'?

Look at audience

19   What kind of person are the advertisers targeting? What sex, what age and job?

20   What sort of magazine or newspaper would the advertisement appear in?

Language in use

NOUNS AND ADJECTIVES

Nouns are words that name objects, places and things.

Adjectives are the describing words that modify the meaning of nouns.

Concrete nouns name objects, *proper nouns* name places and people, and *abstract nouns* name concepts and ideas.

New nouns are constantly emerging, just as old nouns slip out of common usage. 'Aerodrome', 'wireless', 'record player' are all nouns your grandparents would have used, but they sound old fashioned already. 'Videophone', 'compact disc' and 'word-processor' are three new nouns that name recent inventions. They are made in different ways. The first combines the roots of two other words (the Latin word for 'I see' and the Greek word for 'sound'); the second makes a new word from an adjective and a noun, and the third connects two nouns with a hyphen. New product names are often invented in similar ways.

Adjectives provide the fine detail in the language we use. For example, how many different adjectives can you think of that describe something which is new?

Note down the nouns and adjectives in the following passage. Say whether the nouns are concrete, proper or abstract, and use a dictionary to find out their origins.

In the exhibition, visitors can view the latest inventions. These include sophisticated modern satellites that link London with America and provide up-to-date news and instant communications. Also, the introduction of fibre-optic cables means that recent films will soon be available through the telephone. Simply dial a number and the film will appear on your television. An exciting future lies ahead of us all!

7

4 Advertise the future

Now, create your own advertisement. Choose a product from the article at the start of this unit, or imagine a new product for the home of the future. Follow these steps for success.

Step 1

Invent a good name for the product, and a brand name and logo for the company which makes it.

Step 2

What good points of your product will you emphasise?

Step 3

Decide the best way to sell the product: will you advertise in a magazine, or would a leaflet or a pamphlet be a better idea?

Step 4

Decide on your audience.

Step 5

Use the Tips box and glossary to make your advertisement as persuasive as possible.

Step 6

Take special care with layout. The use of illustration is important. Make print eye-catching and make sure that your copy mixes information and persuasion.

Step 7

Use a word-processor or desk-top publishing package to make your advertisement look like the real thing.

A personalised satellite

A walking tea-pot

A 3-D TV set

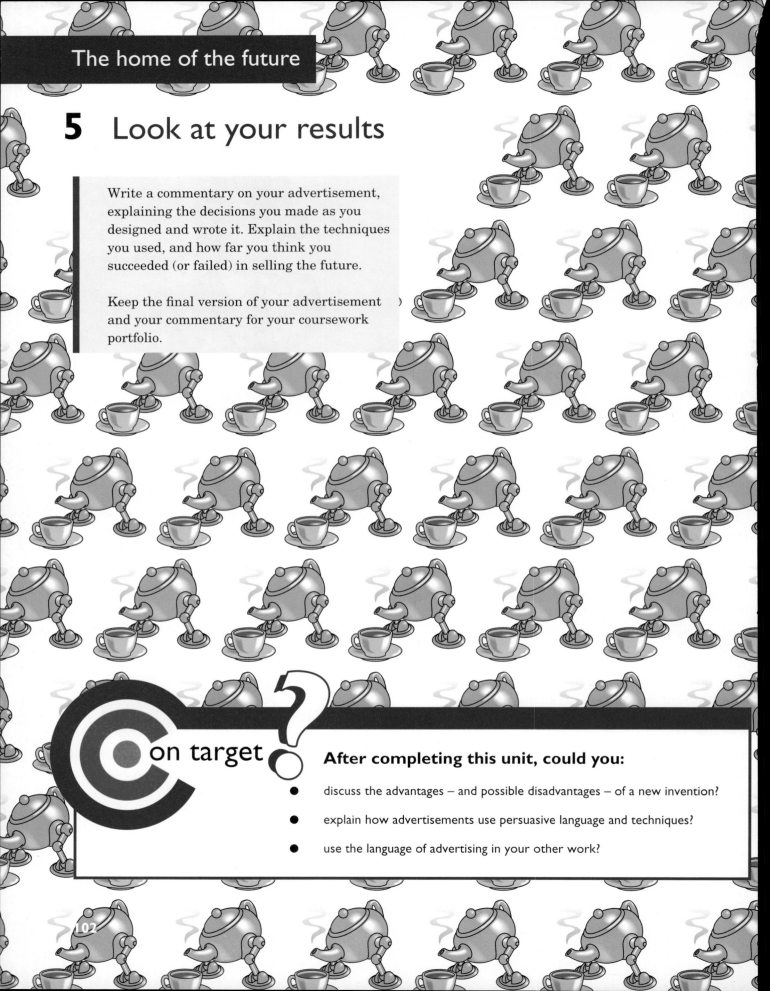

5 Look at your results

Write a commentary on your advertisement, explaining the decisions you made as you designed and wrote it. Explain the techniques you used, and how far you think you succeeded (or failed) in selling the future.

Keep the final version of your advertisement and your commentary for your coursework portfolio.

on target

After completing this unit, could you:

- discuss the advantages – and possible disadvantages – of a new invention?
- explain how advertisements use persuasive language and techniques?
- use the language of advertising in your other work?

Writing

Good writers know what they want to say and who they are writing for. They use writing to communicate their ideas and they adapt how they write to suit their readers. They write to describe, to entertain, to persuade and to offer comment. They write in a range of forms including letters, diaries, stories, scripts and advertising materials. They think hard about paragraphing, punctuation, spelling and handwriting. They always aim to improve in these areas. They try to improve the organisation of their writing and the vocabulary – the words – they use. They keep neat final drafts.

Writing to inform

Newspaper pages

How is a major national newspaper produced? What can the
professionals teach you about producing your own newspaper?

 **In this unit you will look at how a daily newspaper is
produced. You will then have a chance to put what
you have learned into practice by writing and
designing a page of your own newspaper.**

A day in the life of a newspaper

Read the following pages closely to find out how a daily newspaper is produced and to learn about the different jobs of the people who write, edit and design it.

Before you start, read the glossary below.

The language of newspapers – glossary

The Editor, Section Editors and the editorial	The Editor has overall responsibility for all that goes into the paper. He or she writes the *editorial* where the newspaper gives its views on events. Section Editors work under the Editor with responsibility for areas like sport, features, home news, foreign news.
Managing Editors, sub-editors and Night Editor	The Managing Editor has responsibility for producing the paper. Sub-editors work under him or her laying out the pages. The Night Editor takes over at night.
Journalists	Journalists are the people who find the stories. Most work in their own specialist areas. They *file* their stories as text on a computer screen.
Flat-plan	A flat-plan is an outline of the pages of the newspaper used to plan each edition.
Photo opportunities	Photo opportunities are events that are set up by people and businesses who want to publicise what they are doing, or other events that will make an excellent picture.
Advertising departments	Newspapers make more of their money from advertising than from sales. This department has a big say in page layout.
Press conferences	Organisations of all kinds invite journalists to press conferences and give them items of news that they would like them to print.
Features pages	These are sections of a newspaper that are devoted to a particular theme or issue (e.g. music, problem pages, arts).
Masthead	This is the name for the displayed title of a newspaper which appears on the front page.

Newspaper pages

0800

Most journalists start their day by reading their own paper and competing papers. They listen to the news and watch television. Some stories will already have been written. The titles of these are displayed on editors' computer screens. Journalists are ready to be sent off at any time to cover unexpected stories.

0900

The advertising department informs the Managing Editor what space has been sold and how the advertisements will be spread across the paper. Stories from news services come in on screen. A 'copy taster' picks out the more interesting stories, and the Home and Foreign Editors may follow them up. Journalists and photographers cover events that were known about in advance, such as press conferences, court cases and photo opportunities.

1000

Most journalists arrive at the office. Editors for each section of the paper will know by now how much space they have for the day. The Managing Editor has probably set the deadlines for all sections of the paper by now. These deadlines are recorded on a 'flat-plan' of the paper for that day. Features pages have the earliest deadlines; the front page and the sports pages have the latest.

1100

The Editor and the Section Editors meet to decide on some of the possible stories. Each editor presents the stories he or she thinks might be suitable; possible problems are discussed and suggestions made. They try to decide what the editorials will be about.

1200-1300

Journalists use their lunch times to follow up contacts. The majority of the sub-editors begin to arrive. They start to put some of the news pages together.

1400

A lawyer is available in the office. He or she reads all of the stories that will go into the paper to make sure that none of them is libellous. Political journalists begin their coverage of parliamentary proceedings. By this time some pages are already made up.

1500

Stories that 'break' during the day mean that the sub-editors may have to start a page again from scratch.

1600

The first pages for the next day's paper are sent electronically to the printers.

1700

As deadlines approach, more journalists have filed their day's stories, and most of their day's work is done. Sports and political journalists are not so lucky.

1800

Journalists and sub-editors are at their busiest, finishing off stories and putting pages together in time for their deadlines. Usually, Parliament is still in session and most evening sports fixtures are about to begin. The journalists in these two areas work to very tight deadlines.

1900–2100

The bulk of the paper will already have been sent to the printers by now. The business, foreign, home and sports pages will be completing their stories for the first edition. On most days this is the latest time for pages to be sent to the printer. The first and last pages are sent last. Some changes will be made as different editions are printed. The Night Editor will decide on what these changes should be.

2200

On special occasions, such as elections, the front page can be held until now. On other occasions, the paper is printing at this time. The Night Editor, some sub-editors and some journalists will still be working. At any time, a big story can break.

Language in use

SENTENCES AND PHRASES

Sentences are groups of words that make sense when written on their own. Sentences begin with a capital letter and end with a full stop, a question mark or an exclamation mark.

A *phrase* is a group of words that are connected but do not make sense on their own.

Are the underlined sections in the passage below sentences or phrases? Rewrite the passage with capital letters and punctuation marks.

home news stories may be written <u>in the building</u> but journalists may also file their stories using fax, modems, telex and telephone links some <u>software can scan a typewritten page and put it on the computer screen where the paper is laid out</u> pictures can be developed in the building from a photographer's film <u>transmitted electronically to the newspaper</u> or captured from television sources

8

Read the ten statements below. Which are true, and which are false?

List the numbers 1–10. Alongside each number, write 'True', if you think the statement of that number is true, or write your own correct version of the statement, if you think it is false.

1 Journalists work a nine-to-five day.
2 A copy taster is a person who looks out for interesting stories.
3 Newspaper pages are always printed in order.
4 Journalists don't specialise in any one kind of story; they like to cover stories of all kinds.
5 Sub-editors go out each day looking for stories.
6 The sections of the paper are put together as news arrives, to keep them varied.
7 The Editor writes the editorial.
8 Lawyers check that the pages are not slanderous.
9 The features pages are completed first.
10 The front page of a newspaper is never printed before 10.00pm.

Write your own newspaper

Working in groups, write some pages from your own newspaper, based around your school and your local community.

Newspapers are successful if they understand their audiences and print the stories they want to read. So, they spend time researching how to meet their readers' needs.

Talk about what the tastes and interests of *your* audience are likely to be.

Next, decide what pages you would like to produce. Choose from the following: front page, back page, home news, sports news, features or entertainment.

As a group, you can either all focus on one or two kinds of page or else each tackle a separate page – these separate pages can then be put together to make a complete newspaper. Remember that, if you want to add the final page to your coursework portfolio, each person's contribution must be kept separate.

Follow these steps for success.

Step 1 – starting off

Draw up a sketch of your newspaper. Show how much space will be taken up by photos and illustrations, crosswords and other features. Work to an A3 page.

Decide who will do the following jobs, but expect to find yourself doing more than one:

- The *Editor* keeps people to deadlines, has the final say when decisions have to be made and writes the final editorial.
- The *journalists* find, research and write stories.
- The *sub-editors* are responsible for the layout of the paper and for typing in stories. They work with artists (who produce graphs, diagrams, illustrations, cartoons and the paper's masthead) and photographers (who take photos to go with news stories and photos that make stories in themselves).

Professional tip Draw a flat-plan for your paper.

Newspaper pages

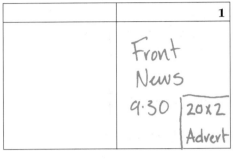
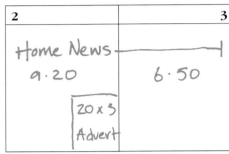
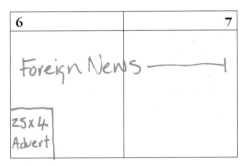
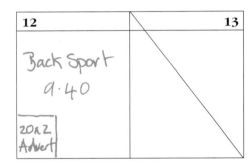
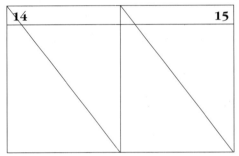

the HERALD   *date*

	1	2	3	4	

Front News 9.30   20x2 Advert

Home News 9.20   6.50   20x3 Advert

Feature 3.10   Advert

| 6 | 7 | 8 | 9 | 10 | 1 |

Foreign News   25x4 Advert

Feature 5.50   Leader 7.30

TV + listings 4.00   Sport 7.40   5x8 Advert

| 12 | 13 | 14 | 15 |

Back Sport 9.40   20x2 Advert

Step 2 – finding stories

Some stories, like school events, can be anticipated, and journalists can be assigned to cover them in advance. Others occur without warning and will need to be investigated – by interviewing witnesses, for instance.

Professional tip   Use local resources. Appoint your own 'copy tasters' to listen to local radio and television news. Scan your local newspapers and cut out interesting articles.

Step 3 – photographs

Photographs should be planned in plenty of time. Photographers should cover school events, find their own stories and accompany journalists on their investigations.

Professional tip   All newspapers use picture libraries. Sometimes the best picture to illustrate your story might be in the school library.

Step 4 – writing and sub-editing

Each member of the team should aim to write at least one article. When you have these in first draft, you can think about the layout of the final paper. You will need to make the following decisions:

- Which story is going to go on the front page?
- Will it need a photograph or picture?
- Is it long enough to fill the whole page, or will there be a second story?
- How are the other pages going to be organised?

Your designers will have made some decisions about general layout, space for headlines and the number of columns you will use. You can now produce a mock-up of how the final paper will look, based on print-outs from your word-processor. Use scissors and glue to paste the stories and illustrations on to an A3 sheet of paper for each page.

Working with the mock-up, the articles can now be sub-edited. Some will have to be cut to fit into the space available, others will have to have further details added if they are not long enough.

Add the headlines. Read each article carefully and think of a headline that sums it up and will attract your readers' attention. Think about how big the headlines should be.

Professional tip   Use sub-headings to fill small amounts of space. These take up three lines: the subheading itself, and the lines before and after.

Step 5 – production

Once the Editor has completed his or her leading article, commenting on some of the issues raised by your paper, you should be ready to go into production. Make sure that your finished pages are neat and well presented.

... on using desk-top publishing

Choose a clear *typeface* and set a narrow *ruler* so that your writing comes out in columns that you can cut and paste on to your mock-up.

Think about text effects. Look at how the columns can be *justified* – made neat at the right-hand edge. Think about a *first-line* indent to start each paragraph.

Some desk-top publishing programs allow you to write in columns. With these you may be able to produce a section of the page at a time, leaving space for illustrations. You may also be able to *scan* images and artwork on to the page.

Remember that *white space* on pages is important if the final version is to be clear and easy to read.

... on writing journalism

The shape below is known as the 'journalist's triangle'. It shows how, in news journalism, the most important information comes first, followed by the more detailed explanation; finally, if space permits, the story includes examples and odds and ends of information. This 'triangle' allows a story to be cut from the end in order to fit a space. Use the same pattern in your own writing.

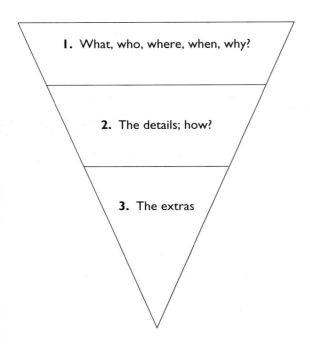

1. What, who, where, when, why?

2. The details; how?

3. The extras

1　A broken fire alarm led to an emergency evacuation of St Andrew's School on Tuesday afternoon.

2　Three fire engines arrived within minutes of the alarm being raised, but already the 600 pupils had been evacuated on to the playground. Headteacher, Jemima Rood, blamed a faulty electrical circuit for the emergency and praised the teachers and the pupils for their calm.

3　One pupil, Kevin Watson (13), slightly sprained his ankle on the stairs.

Evaluate your newspaper

Review the newspapers produced by the class by handing out journalistic awards.

First, display all the newspapers. Then, vote for, and choose, a prize-winner in each of the following categories:

- Best single article
- Best layout
- Most promising young journalist
- Best news feature
- Best overall newspaper.

After completing this unit, could you:

- describe some of the ways in which newspaper stories come to be written?

- write about the process by which you produced your own newspaper?

- give advice to a student in another class about the best way to put a newspaper together?

Enough is enough.

FRIENDS *of the*
earth

Writing to report

Caring for the planet

Every day we throw away tons of plastic, glass, paper and metal which could be recycled with the right equipment. But, while recycling helps to conserve the earth's resources, building a recycling plant might bring some unwelcome changes.

In this unit you will discuss whether the site proposed for a new recycling plant is suitable. You will read information about the problem and about the proposed site. Finally, you will write a report of your investigations and conclusions.

The problem of waste

Read the article below.

Conserving scarce resources

If we consider energy, water and other elements, we can see how we need to make better use of our resources. We have enough and to spare, provided we are less *profligate* in our ways. Fortunately, there is massive scope for us to improve. The challenge lies not so much with 'technical fixes', but with our approach to the world around us.

In the past, we have engaged in something of a Wild West economy, supposing that there are always pastures new beyond the horizon. Now we know there are no new horizons to explore and exploit: our planet is a closed *ecosystem*. So, a more appropriate image is Earth as a spaceship, where most materials have to be recycled. That means leaving behind the throwaway society and advancing to a 'conserver society'. To qualify as citizens of a conserver society, we must shift *entrenched* attitudes and thinking. We need to recognise that there is rarely such a thing as 'waste': rather there are materials that sometimes end up in the wrong place.

The *transition* has already begun. Recycling a glass container saves only 8 per cent; but in parts of the US, a citizen buying a bottle of soda or beer now pays a deposit against return of the empty bottle. If all drinks containers in the US were to be re-used, the annual savings would amount to 0.5

million tonnes of glass – plus almost 50 million barrels of oil used in production processes.

In Japan, the mounting price of oil spurred an increase in recycling of raw materials from 16 per cent to 48 per cent in just five years. In Norway, the price of a new car now includes a disposal cost of about $100, redeemable when the junked car is turned in at an approved receiving centre. The *thrifty* Chinese claim they re-use 2.5 million tonnes of scrap iron each year, and at least one million tonnes of waste paper.

All this recycling also helps with the problem of waste disposal. An average American generates about one tonne of waste each year. To get rid of this garbage, the US uses almost 15,000 landfill and other sites – an area of some 200,000 hectares. In the main, the conserver society depends on the *commitment* of individuals. But they can be inspired by government *incentives* and penalties.

Once the 'usable' rubbish has been separated, it still leaves the problem of what to do with the rest. Burning domestic waste has several obvious advantages. It leaves only harmless ash to be disposed of, and the furnace can be used to produce heat and electricity. But it has its drawbacks too, like those associated with industrial *incineration*. The smoke produced may be unpleasant or even *toxic*, and it may be more expensive than landfill.

In Denmark, Japan, Sweden and Switzerland, about half of household waste is now burned, producing steam which is used by industry or for heating nearby houses. A better way to *extract* energy from waste may be to dump it in a landfill site and allow it to rot down. The process produces methane gas, which can be tapped off through pipes and used to provide fuel for factories or power stations. Worthwhile amounts of methane can be generated from ordinary rubbish, and landfill sites are now being designed with this in mind.

Answer the following questions, using your own words:

a Describe the difference between a 'Wild West' approach and a 'Spaceship' approach to the earth's resources.

b Write about how the following groups can help to stop 'the throwaway society':
   – individual householders;
   – industries.
   – governments;

c Find words or phrases that could replace the ten words in italics in the article.

d Describe how resources can be created from waste which is not suitable for recycling.

e Summarise the damage that can be caused to the environment by recycling processes.

A suitable site for a recycling plant?

Working with a group, you are now going to look at how environmental issues are presented to the public. First, read this newspaper article and study the map and the planning proposal on pages 118–119.

Waste plant for Fordham?

Ms Norma Brown, Chair of British Waste Disposal Ltd., was on a fact-finding mission in Fordham yesterday. Her visit to the area surrounding the recently demolished Manor Farm left a question mark hanging over the future development of local countryside. She revealed that she was investigating possible sites for a major new waste recycling development.

Plans for development

BWDL plan to build a waste recycling plant on the open-field site. They intend to take waste materials from all over Britain, and possibly Europe, to reclaim valuable raw materials by recycling.

Boom

Councillor Hugh Wadham told us, 'This could be the beginning of a boom time. A recycling plant will create jobs, attract more industry to the area, and help us do our bit for conservation.' Beech Wood resident, Hannah Green, spoke for many when she commented, 'I bought my house because of its beautiful views. I don't want ugly buildings and noisy roads built around here.'

Threat

A spokesperson for Friends of the Planet, Gail Thorpe, expressed concern about the effect the proposed building might have on local wildlife. 'Many rare meadow flowers can be found in this area, such as meadow saffron and crane's bill. It is also a nesting site for birds, including the barn owl.' She went on to emphasise the serious threat to many endangered species if building goes ahead.

1   Excellent rail links to south, east, west and north, including major cities, ports and Channel Tunnel
2   The road links reinforce the rail system
3   The town: home to unskilled labour force and skilled scientists, technicians, etc.
4   Large open-field site – Manor Farm
5   River Kennet – Angling Club buildings
6   Residential area: schools, houses and hospitals

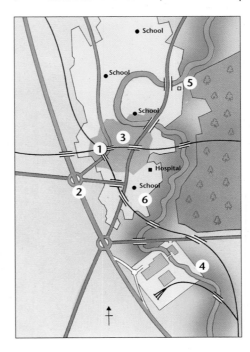

In the next part of this unit, each one of you will represent the point of view of a different group. You can be:

– A senior employee of British Waste Disposal Limited, concerned with the advantages of the site for your new recycling plant.

– A member of Friends of the Planet, concerned to prevent damage to the environment.

– A representative of the Local Residents' Association, concerned that the neighbourhood should not be spoiled.

– A representative of the local Chamber of Commerce, concerned with the advantages and disadvantages for local industries.

Choose the role you will play. Look back over the materials and make some notes about your point of view. Then, hold a group discussion where you have one minute to explain what you think about the proposed plan.

The plans for development proposed by British Waste Disposal Limited (BWDL)

They want to build a waste recycling unit on the open-field site. They intend to take waste materials from all over Britain, and possibly Europe, to reclaim valuable raw materials by recycling.

Key

A Depot – a new rail line will deliver materials to be stored here until required.

B Separation unit – the waste materials will be separated into four main categories: plastic, glass, paper and metal.

C Glass unit – the glass will be sorted into different colours, then broken up to make cullet, a raw material used to produce new glass. This material will be sold to the glass-making industry.

D Paper unit – paper will be broken up in water from the Kennet to make pulp. This will be treated to remove unwanted materials, then sold to make new paper or cardboard. Water will be filtered before being pumped back into the river.

E Metals unit – advanced refining methods will retrieve aluminium, iron, steel, copper, gold plating and silver.

F Plastics unit – these will be taken from the separation unit for redistribution.

G Redistribution and transport – recycled products will be stored here until sold. A fleet of vehicles will be available for transport.

H Social club – a leisure complex for the use of BWDL employees and their families.

I Administration block – managers, administrators and clerical staff. Reception area for visitors to the site.

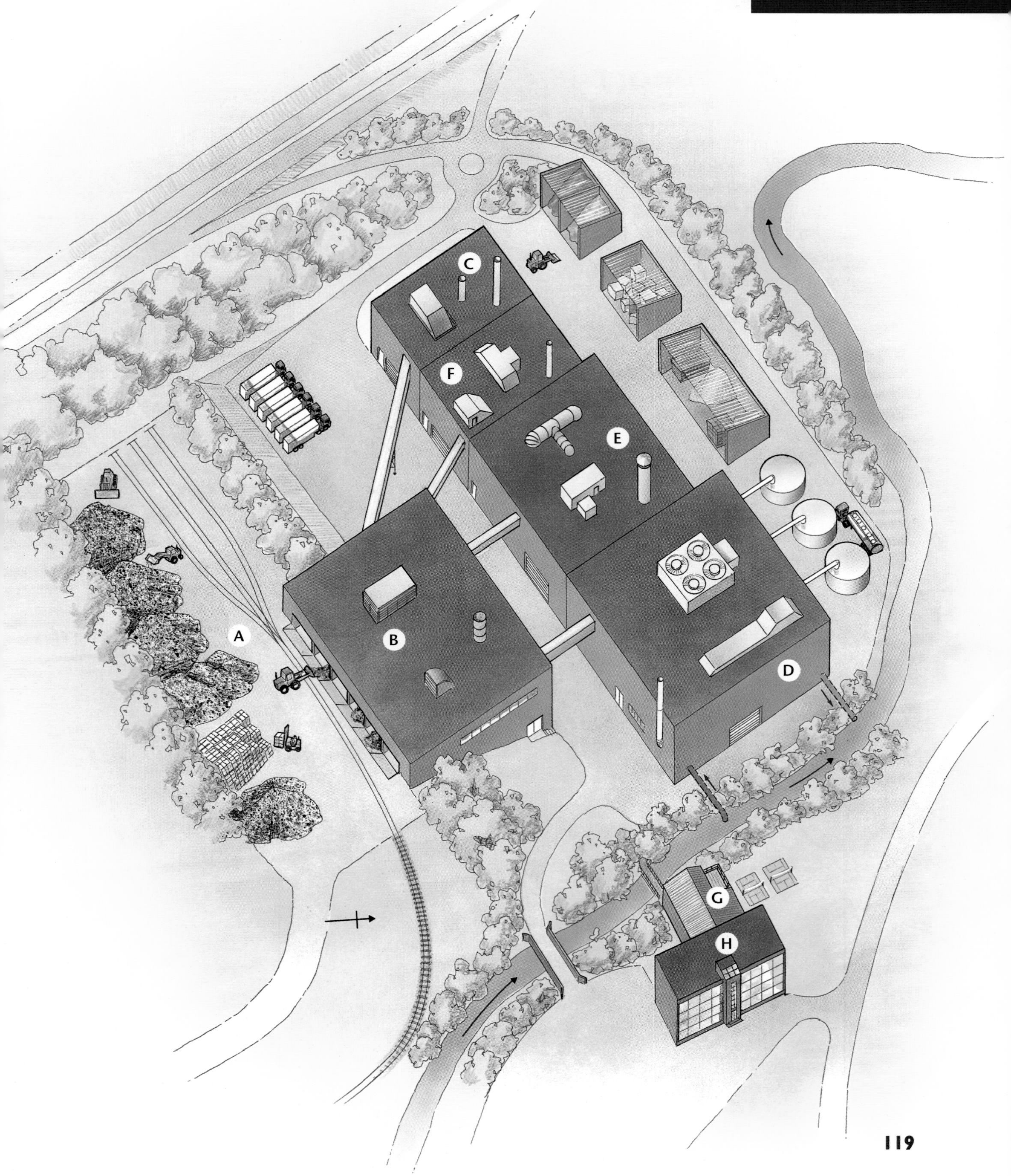
C
F
E
B
A
D
G
H

3 Write a report

Now, imagine that you have been asked to write a report about the Waste Recycling Plan proposals for the group you represent. Your terms of reference (the instructions about the aims of your report and what it should cover) are set out below.

Friends of the Planet

Terms of reference

1   To provide detailed ground plans of the present site and the proposed site.

2   To explain the purpose of the proposed site.

3   To describe the possible dangers to the community and environment, should such a site be built.

4   To suggest ways in which Friends of the Planet can dissuade BWDL from building.

The Chamber of Commerce

Terms of reference

1   To provide detailed ground plans of the present site and the proposed site.

2   To explain the purpose of the proposed site.

3   To describe the advantages to local industry if the recycling plant is built.

4   To suggest how the Chamber of Commerce can support BWDL in overcoming local objections to the building.

BRITISH WASTE DISPOSAL LIMITED

Terms of reference

1.   To provide detailed ground plans of the present site and the proposed site.
2.   To explain the advantages of this particular site for BWDL.
3.   To assess the possible problems arising from building a unit on this site. To provide background information about local opinion.
4.   To suggest ways in which any problems can be resolved.

The Beech Wood Residents' Association

Terms of reference

1   To provide detailed ground plans of the present site and the proposed site.
2   To explain the purpose of the proposed site.
3   To describe the advantages and disadvantages to local residents if the recycling plant is built.
4   To suggest future action the Residents' Association should take, either to dissuade BWDL from building the plant or to persuade BWDL to change plans to benefit local residents.

Keep a copy of the terms of reference and your finished report for your coursework portfolio.

... on report writing

The purpose of a report and the nature of the audience you are writing for are, usually, identified for you. You have to structure your writing carefully to meet this purpose and audience. You need to think about what your readers know already and what they need to know.

When you write a report, you need to:

research: find out as much as you can about the subject

evaluate: think about the information and about what the consequences are likely to be, and select the most important facts

write: write up the information in a clear and organised way

recommend: make suggestions based on the information.

The six sections of a report are:

1   *The title* which should be short and give a clear indication of the subject.

2   The *terms of reference* which explain what you have been asked to do. This section should include:
- who the report is for
- an outline of the information you have been asked to find
- a description of how and where you found the information.

3   The *findings* where you provide factual information. You may need to do more research in reference books to complete this section. Charts and drawings may be better than writing.

4   The *conclusion* where you sum up the main points of your findings.

5   The *recommendations* where you give your opinion and make suggestions about how to deal with problems or what to do next.

6   The *ending* where your report is signed and dated.

You may need to include maps or diagrams. Don't forget that accuracy is essential when you are presenting factual information or writing for the public and how your report looks will influence how people receive it.

Language in use

FORMS OF WRITING

A report is one type of writing with its
own shape and features. Narratives,
poems and scripts are other writing types.

This chart compares some of the features
of reports and narratives.

Features	In reports	In narratives
What is the purpose for writing?	To investigate an issue and present findings.	To entertain or stimulate.
Who is the writing for?	A specified audience.	A broad group of possible readers.
Is the structure of the writing chronological (describing events in the order in which they happened)?	No.	Yes.
Is the structure discursive (discussing events under headings or topics)?	Yes.	No.
Does the writing build up to a climax?	No.	Yes.
Are examples given?	Yes.	No.
Are sub-headings used?	Yes.	No.
Is conversation used?	No.	Yes.
Does the writing use comparisons?	No.	Yes.
Is there more factual language than anything else in the writing?	Yes.	No.
Does the writing use descriptive language?	No.	Yes.

9

Use similar questions to create a chart that
compares a magazine article with a
playscript.

Present your report

Prepare a talk which summarises your findings and present it to the rest of your class. Organise what you want to say and link it to the structure of your report. Use maps, diagrams and overhead projector transparencies to illustrate your points.

Afterwards, as a class, discuss the points of view raised. Decide whether BWDL should be allowed to go ahead with their plans or whether the plans should be revised or abandoned.

 on target

After working through this unit, could you:

- take part in a debate about the effect of recycling waste products on the environment?

- explain to a friend how the style and organisation of a report differ from other types of writing?

- research and write a report on another issue?

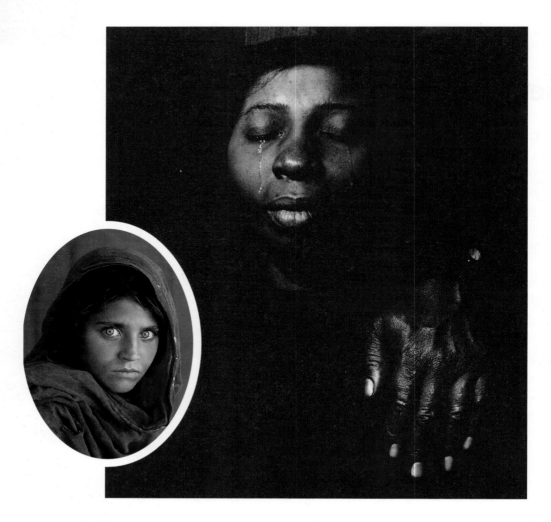

Writing to describe

Pictures of people

Characterisation is at the heart of fiction. Some people claim to know characters from books and plays better than people from real life. How do authors approach the problem of making their characters 'come to life'?

In this unit you will look at the ways in which writers describe characters. You will investigate their techniques and learn to use them in your own writing.

Look at people

Study the faces below.

For each photograph, write down what the picture suggests to you about the person. Briefly describe the character and guess at his age, occupation, personality or character. Write a few sentences about his daily life.

Working as a small group, compare your ideas. See whether you agree.

Next, agree on three new pieces of information that would help you come to some better conclusions about the characters. Report back to the class.

2 Analyse characters in literature

Read the extracts below.

Maureen Peal

This disrupter of seasons was a new girl in school named Maureen Peal. A high-yellow dream child with long brown hair braided into two lynch ropes that hung down her back. She was rich, at least by our standards, as rich as the richest of the white girls, swaddled in comfort and care. The quality of her clothes threatened to derange Frieda and me. Patent-leather shoes with buckles, a cheaper version of which we got only at Easter and which had disintegrated by the end of May. Fluffy sweaters the color of lemon drops tucked into skirts with pleats so orderly they astounded us. Brightly colored knee socks with white borders, a brown velvet coat trimmed in white rabbit fur, and a matching muff. There was a hint of spring in her sloe green eyes, something summery in her complexion, and a rich autumn ripeness in her walk.

She enchanted the entire school. When teachers called on her, they smiled encouragingly. Black boys didn't trip her in the halls; white boys didn't stone her, white girls didn't suck their teeth when she was assigned to be their work partners; black girls stepped aside when she wanted to use the sink in the girls' toilet, and their eyes genuflected under sliding lids. She never had to search for anybody to eat with in the cafeteria – they flocked to the table of her choice, where she opened fastidious lunches, shaming our jelly-stained bread with egg-salad sandwiches cut into four dainty squares, pink-frosted cupcakes, sticks of celery and carrots, proud, dark apples. She even bought and liked white milk.

Toni Morrison (from The Bluest Eye)

Eva

Sitting behind Eva and Dad in the car, watching their hands constantly fluttering towards each other, you didn't have to be a genius to see they were a couple. Here before me were two people in love, oh yes. And as Eva drove, Dad didn't take his eyes from her face.

This woman I barely knew, Eva, had stolen my father. But what did I really think of her? I hadn't even looked at her properly.

This new part of my life wasn't a woman who would seem attractive straight-on in a passport photograph. She had no conventional beauty, her features were not exquisitely proportioned and her face was a bit chubby. But she was lovely because the round face with the straight dyed-blonde hair, which fell over her forehead and into her eyes, was open. Her face was constantly in motion, and this was the source of her beauty. Her face registered the slightest feeling, concealing little. Sometimes she became childlike and you could see her at eight or seventeen or twenty-five. The different ages of her life seemed to exist simultaneously, as if she could move from age to age according to how she felt. There was no cold maturity about her, thank Christ. She could be pretty serious and honest, though, explaining hurt and pain as if we were all openly human like her, and not screwed-up and secretive and tricky. That time she'd told me how lonely and abandoned she felt when she was with her husband, those confessional words, 'lonely and abandoned', which usually would have me cringing all over the place, made me shiver.

When she was ecstatic, and she was often ecstatic, ecstasy flew from her face like the sun from a mirror. She was living outwardly, towards you, and her face was always watchable because she was rarely bored or dull. She didn't let the world bore her. And she was some talker, old Eva.

Hanif Kureishi (from The Buddha of Suburbia)

The old woman

The old woman sat playing solitaire, hearing the quiet click of her wedding-ring on the polished table top each time she laid her hand flat to study the ranks of cards. They were never right. Never worked out. A crucial king face down, buried – and the game was lost. She realised how futile it was – not only this particular game but the activity of playing solitaire, and yet she could not stop herself, so she dealt the cards again. They flipped down silently, cushioned as they slid on the shine of the wood. She was reluctant to cheat. She played maybe six times before she gave up, put the cards away and sat gnawing her thumbnail. Perhaps later, left alone, it would come out.

She moved to the kitchen and took her magnesia, not bothering with the spoon but slugging the blue bottle back, hearing the white liquid tilt thickly. She swallowed hard, holding her thrapple. She stopped breathing through her nose so as not to taste, and held her mouth open. She walked to the bedroom, still breathing through her mouth until she saw herself in the mirror with crescents of white at the sides of her open lips. When she closed her teeth she heard and felt the sand of the magnesia grate between them. Her skin was loose and wrinkled, hanging about the bones she knew to be beneath her face. There were crows' feet at the corners of her eyes. With one finger she pressed down beneath her eye, baring its red sickle. They watered too much when the weather was cold. She wiped the white from the sides of her mouth with a tissue and began dressing, putting on several layers against the cold, with her old cardigan on top. She combed her white hair back from her forehead and looked at the number of hairs snagged on the comb. She removed them and with a fidget of her fingers dropped them into the waste-paper basket.

Bernard MacLaverty (from *Eels*)

Mary Fisher

Mary Fisher lives in a High Tower, on the edge of the sea: she writes a great deal about the nature of love. She tells lies.

Mary Fisher is forty-three, and accustomed to love. There has always been a man around to love her, sometimes quite desperately, and she has on occasion returned this love, but never, I think, with desperation. She is a writer of romantic fiction. She tells lies to herself, and to the world.

Mary Fisher has $(US) 754,300 on deposit in a bank in Cyprus, where the tax laws are lax. This is the equivalent of £502,867 sterling, 1,931,009 Deutschmark, 1,599,117 Swiss francs, 185,055,050 yen and so forth, it hardly matters which. A woman's life is what it is, in any corner of the world. And wherever you go it is the same – to those who hath, such as Mary Fisher, shall be given, and to those who hath not, such as myself, even that which they have shall be taken away.

Mary Fisher earned all her money herself. Her first husband, Jonah, told her that capitalism was immoral, and she believed him, having a gentle and pliable nature. Otherwise no doubt by now Mary Fisher would have a substantial portfolio of investments. As it is, she owns four houses and these are cumulatively worth – depending on the state of the property market – anything between half a million and a million dollars. A house, of course, only means anything in financial terms if there is anyone to buy it, or if you can bear to sell it. Otherwise a house can only be somewhere to live, or somewhere where those connected with you can live. With luck the ownership of property brings peace of mind; without this luck it brings aggravation and discontent. I wish un-luck in property matters on Mary Fisher.

Mary Fisher is small and pretty and delicately formed, prone to fainting and weeping and sleeping with men while pretending that she doesn't.

Mary Fisher is loved by my husband, who is her accountant.

I love my husband and I hate Mary Fisher.

Fay Weldon (from *The Life and Loves of a She-Devil*)

Jennifer

Dear Ben Joe:

We received yours of the 12th. Yes, of course we are all well. I don't know why you keep asking us, since you know as well as we do that the last time any of us was in the hospital was five years ago when Susannah had all four wisdom teeth pulled at once. Mama says to tell you you worry too much. We are getting along beautifully & hope you are too.

Financially things are going smoothly. Next month both of the twins are getting raises at the bank, but Lisa is getting $6 more a month than Jane, which make family relationships kind of tense. Tessie is taking drawing lessons after school now for $2 a lesson, which I think we can afford, & the only extra expense this month has been the eaves pipe falling down from the roof outside Tessie's & my window due to Tessie's standing on it. Tessie didn't, tho. Fall, I mean. I'll never know why.

I wish you would write a letter to the family suggesting that we go back to the policy of my doing the grocery shopping. Specially since it was me you left in charge of the money. Gram has been doing it lately & the results are disaster. She gets anything she feels like, minced clams and pickled artichoke hearts & pig's feet & when I ask where are the meat & potatoes she says it's time we had a little change around here. She's ruining us.

Enclosed is next month's check for your expenses, etc. I hope you will remember to send a receipt this time as it makes my bookkeeping neater.

Sincerely,

Encl.   Jennifer

Anne Tyler (from *If Morning Ever Comes*)

Make a brief assessment of the five characters.

For each character, note down your answers to these questions:

- What facts have you discovered about her?
- What have you found out about her appearance?
- What have you found out about her life?
- What impression have you formed of her?
- Who is describing her? Could this make a difference to the description?

Make a copy of the chart below to help you.

The character	Maureen Peel	Eva	The old woman	Mary Fisher	Jennifer
Facts about her					
How her appearance is described					
Her life					
Overall impression					
Who tells the story					

... on narrative technique

First-person and *third-person narratives* are the commonest ways to present a character in a story.

A *first-person*, or *'I' narrative*, is one in which the character speaks directly to the reader or audience. In this kind of writing:

- the central character has to witness all the events of the story;

- the reader only knows what the character chooses to tell;

- the thoughts and feelings of the narrator make the writing immediate and exciting;

- the way the story unfolds through the narrator's eyes makes the writing authentic.

A *third-person narrative* is one in which the narrator is not a part of the story, but tells it from the 'outside'. In this kind of writing:

- the author can report the thoughts and feelings of anyone in the story – this can lead to a fuller understanding of complicated situations;

- the author is free to tell the story from several different angles or can shift easily from one set of characters to another;

- it can be harder for a reader to get involved with the characters;

- the writing can seem less realistic than the first-person point of view.

Pictures of people

Choose two, or three, of the extracts and write a detailed comparison of the way they describe the characters. Comment on how the writers:

- choose a point of view from which to describe their characters;
- use adjectives, comparisons and factual statements to describe the characters;
- give an impression of the characters' lives by describing things they do or have done;
- use other characters to help create their impression;
- use language and select the vocabulary that best describes their characters.

Language in use

CONNECTIVES

Detailed descriptions need *connectives* (linking words) to join sentences and clauses and make the writing read fluently. In your own writing, aim to use a variety of connectives to produce the complex sentences that communicate your meaning and show that you are an accomplished writer.

- *Prepositions* go before nouns and noun phrases to show their positions in either space or time. For example:

From *under* the jutting eyebrows two sharp eyes *with* a piercing blue glint to them stared *across* the room.

- *Co-ordinating conjunctions* ('and', 'but' and 'or') join sentences together. *Subordinating conjunctions* (words like 'when', 'if', 'although') show that one clause is part of another. For example:

Her hair was fair *and* her skin was starting to tan. *Although* she had been in Florida for only a week, the sun had done its best to add to her beauty.

- *Adverbial clauses and phrases* work like adverbs to answer the questions, 'When?' 'How?' and 'Where?' about a verb. For example:

After she finished her lunch, the old lady hobbled into the garden and dug at the weeds in the borders *with her trowel*.

- *Pronouns*, the short words that take the place of nouns (words like 'his', 'mine', 'some') also link descriptive writing. For example:

The man in the gymnasium had been working out for some time, and *his* forehead was wet with the sweat that dripped from *his* hairline.

3 Create your own character

Create your own character using some of the techniques explored in this unit.

Follow these steps for success.

Step 1
Think of a context for your character
Your character cannot exist in isolation so make notes on his or her life so far. Think about the character's family, relationships, home and work. Think of unusual things that may have happened to him or her.

Step 2
Think about your character
Give him or her a distinguishing feature – physical or mental – that will help you get started. Think of some striking aspect of his or her appearance. Ask yourself what would be the first thing that someone would notice about this character.

Step 3
Decide at what point in his or her life you are going to describe the character
He or she might be starting out on a new phase in his or her life, arriving in a new place, meeting new people or facing up to an important decision.

Step 4
Draft your character portrait
Choose one narrative technique and stick to it. Think about how to show inward feelings as well as giving a physical impression of your character.

Step 5
Revise carefully
Add description at this stage. Ask yourself what is unlikely about the character. Imagine your character in front of you and think about what you have left out in writing about him or her.

Step 6
Write a neat final version

on target

After completing this unit, could you:

- describe at least two methods of creating a character to the class?

- include more interesting and realistic characters in your writing?

- comment on how an author present characters in a book or play you are studying?

Writing to excite

Tense times

What makes a story exciting? What keeps you, as a reader, on the edge of your seat? How can you introduce more excitement and tension into your own writing?

In this unit you will look at how to produce writing which is tense and exciting by exploring how other writers achieve their effects.

Using structure to create tension

The passage below is taken from *Dracula* by Bram Stoker. The vampire hunters have tracked down a vampire, Lucy, to her resting place. The hunters are: Professor Van Helsing, an expert on vampires; Arthur, the vampire's former fiancé; Quincey, Arthur's friend and Dr Seward, the narrator.

Read the extract carefully.

An infinite kindness

He unlocked the door, and we entered, closing it behind us. Then he took from his bag the lantern, which he lit, and also two wax candles, which, when lighted, he stuck, by melting their own ends, on other coffins, so that they might give light sufficient to work by. When he again lifted the lid off Lucy's coffin we all looked – Arthur trembling like an aspen – and saw that the body lay there in all its death-beauty. But there was no love in my own heart, nothing but loathing for the foul Thing which had taken Lucy's shape without her soul. I could see even Arthur's face grow hard as he looked. Presently he said to Van Helsing:

'Is this really Lucy's body, or only a demon in her shape?'

'It is her body, and yet not it. But wait a while, and you shall see her as she was, and is.'

She seemed like a nightmare of Lucy as she lay there; the pointed teeth, the bloodstained, voluptuous mouth – which it made one shudder to see – the whole carnal and unspiritual appearance, seeming like a devilish mockery of Lucy's sweet purity. Van Helsing, in his methodical manner, began taking the various contents from his bag and placing them ready

for use. First he took out a soldering iron and some plumbing solder, and then a small oil-lamp, which gave out, when lit in a corner of the tomb, gas which burned at fierce heat with a blue flame; then his operating knives, which he placed to hand; and last a round wooden stake, some two and a half or three inches thick and about three feet long. One end of it was hardened by charring in the fire, and was sharpened to a fine point. With this stake came a heavy hammer, such as in households is used in the coal-cellar for breaking the lumps. To me, a doctor's preparations for work of any kind are stimulating and bracing, but the effect of these things on both Arthur and Quincey was to cause them a sort of consternation. They both, however, kept their courage, and remained silent and quiet.

When all was ready, Van Helsing said:

'Before we do anything, let me tell you this; it is out of the lore and experience of the ancients and of all those who have studied the powers of the Un-Dead. When they become such, there comes with the change the curse of immortality; they cannot die, but must go on age after age adding new victims and multiplying the evils of the world; for all that die from the preying of the Un-Dead become themselves Un-Dead, and prey on their kind. And so the circle goes on ever widening, like as the ripples from a stone thrown in the water. Friend Arthur, if you had met that kiss which you know of before poor Lucy die; or again, last night when you open your arms to her, you would in time, when you had died, have become *nosferatu*, as they call it in Eastern Europe, and would all time make more of those Un-Deads that so have filled us with horror. The career of this so unhappy dear lady is but just begun. Those children whose blood she suck are not as yet so much the worse; but if she live on, Un-Dead, more and more they lose their blood, and by her power over them they come to her; and so she draw their blood with that so wicked mouth. But if she die in truth, then all cease; the tiny wounds of the throats disappear, and they go back to their plays unknowing ever of what has been. But of the most blessed of all, when this now Un-Dead be made to rest as true dead, then the soul of the poor lady whom we love shall again be free. Instead of working wickedness by night and growing more debased in the assimilation of it by day, she shall take her place with the other Angels. So that, my friend, it will be a blessed hand for her that shall strike the blow that sets her free. To this I am willing; but is there none amongst us who has a better right? Will it be no joy to think of hereafter in the silence of the night when sleep is not: "It was my hand that sent her to the stars; it was the hand of him that loved her best; the hand that of all she would herself have chosen, had it been to her to choose"? Tell me if there be such a one amongst us.'

We all looked at Arthur. He saw, too, what we all did, the infinite kindness, which suggested that his should be the hand which would restore Lucy to us as a holy, and not an unholy, memory; he stepped forward and said bravely, though his hand trembled, and his face was as pale as snow:

'My true friend, from the bottom of my broken heart I thank you. Tell me what I am to do, and I shall not falter!' Van Helsing laid a hand on his shoulder, and said:

'Brave lad! A moment's courage, and it is done. This stake must be driven through her. It will be a fearful ordeal – be not deceived in that – but it will be only a short time, and you will then rejoice more than your pain was great; from this grim tomb you will emerge as though you tread on air. But you must not falter when once you have begun. Only think that we, your true friends, are round you, and that we pray for you all the time.'

'Go on,' said Arthur hoarsely. 'Tell me what I am to do.'

'Take this stake in your left hand, ready to place the point over the heart, and the hammer in your right.

Then when we begin our prayer for the dead – I shall read him; I have here the book, and the others shall follow – strike in God's name, that so all may be well with the dead that we love, and that the Un-Dead pass away.'

Arthur took the stake and the hammer, and when once his mind was set on action his hands never trembled nor even quivered. Van Helsing opened his missal and began to read, and Quincey and I followed as well as we could. Arthur placed the point over the heart, and as I looked I could see its dint in the white flesh. Then he struck with all his might.

The Thing in the coffin writhed; and a hideous blood-curdling screech came from the opened red lips. The body shook and quivered and twisted in wild contortions; the sharp white teeth champed together till the lips were cut and the mouth was smeared with a crimson foam. But Arthur never faltered. He looked like a figure of Thor as his untrembling arm rose and fell, driving deeper and deeper the mercy-bearing stake, whilst the blood from the pierced heart welled and spurted up around it. His face was set, and high duty seemed to shine through it; the sight of it gave us courage, so that our voices seemed to ring through the little vault.

And then the writhing and quivering of the body became less, and the teeth ceased to champ, and the face to quiver. Finally it lay still. The terrible task was over.

The hammer fell from Arthur's hand. He reeled and would have fallen had we not caught him. The great drops of sweat sprang out on his forehead, and his breath came in broken gasps. It had indeed been an awful strain on him; and had he not been forced to his task by more than human considerations he could never have gone through with it. For a few minutes we were so taken up with him that we did not look towards the coffin. When we did, however, a murmur of startled surprise ran from one to the

other of us. We gazed so eagerly that Arthur rose, for he had been seated on the ground, and came and looked too; and then a glad, strange light broke over his face and dispelled altogether the gloom of horror that lay upon it.

There in the coffin lay no longer the foul Thing that we had so dreaded and grown to hate that the work of her destruction was yielded as a privilege to the one best entitled to it, but Lucy as we had seen her in her life, with her face of unequalled sweetness and purity. True that there was there, as we had seen them in life, the traces of care and pain and waste; but these were all dear to us, for they marked her truth to what we knew. One and all we felt that the holy calm that lay like sunshine over the wasted face and form was only an earthly token and symbol of the calm that was to reign for ever.

Van Helsing came and laid his hand on Arthur's shoulder, and said to him:

'And now, Arthur, my friend, dear lad, am I not forgiven?'

The reaction of the terrible strain came as he took the old man's hand in his, and raising it to his lips, pressed it, saying:

'Forgiven! God bless you that you have given my dear one her soul again, and me peace.' He put his hands on the Professor's shoulder, and laying his head on his breast, cried for a while silently, whilst we stood unmoving. When he raised his head Van Helsing said to him:

'And now, my child, you may kiss her. Kiss her dead lips if you will, as she would have you to, if for her to choose. For she is not a grinning devil now – not any more a foul Thing for all eternity. No longer she is the devil's Un-Dead. She is God's true dead, whose soul is with Him!'

Arthur bent and kissed her, and then we sent him and Quincey out of the tomb; the Professor and I

sawed the top off the stake, leaving the point of it in the body. Then we cut off the head and filled the mouth with garlic. We soldered up the leaden coffin, screwed on the coffin-lid, and gathering up our belongings, came away. When the Professor locked the door he gave the key to Arthur.

Outside the air was sweet, the sun shone, and the birds sang, and it seemed as if all nature were turned to a different pitch. There was gladness and mirth and peace everywhere, for we were at rest ourselves on one account, and we were glad, though it was with a tempered joy.

Before we moved away Van Helsing said:

'Now, my friends, one step of our work is done, one of the most harrowing to ourselves. But there remains a greater task: to find out the author of all this our sorrow and to stamp him out. I have clues which we can follow; but it is a long task, and a difficult one, and there is danger in it, and pain. Shall you not all help me? We have learned to believe, all of us – is it not so? And since so, do we not see our duty? Yes! And do we not promise to go on to the bitter end?'

Each in turn, we took his hand, and the promise was made.

Bram Stoker (from *Dracula*)

This list gives the events of the extract, but in a confused order. Make a numbered list of the events in their correct order.

- Arthur recovers and kisses Lucy.
- They agree to help Van Helsing in his pursuit of Dracula.
- The body is restored to its former shape.
- Arthur decides to kill Lucy.
- Van Helsing gives Arthur instructions.
- They go outside into the sunlight.
- Arthur faints from the horror he has witnessed.
- Van Helsing explains how vampires exist.
- Van Helsing and Seward (the narrator) cut off the vampire's head.
- The death of the vampire.
- Van Helsing prepares to kill the vampire.

Decide whether each event is part of the build-up, the climax or the release. Use the Tips box and a copy of the chart below to help you.

... on exciting writing

Exciting writing often consists of a *build-up*, a *climax* and a *release*. In the build-up, events take place that you know are leading up to a dramatic ending, or climax. The release is where the tension lifts, after the climax.

Compare the descriptions of the vampire's death and the cutting off of its head. Why is the first more detailed than the second? Which is the climax of the extract?

Look at the section which begins, 'When all was ready, Van Helsing said ...'. Why does the author interrupt the action like this? What effect does this information have on the way you view the events that follow?

Order	Event	Build-up, climax or release?
1		
2		
3		
4		
5		
6		
7		
8		
9		
10		
11		

2 Using language to create tension

Read the following passage from *The Handmaid's Tale* by Margaret Atwood. Offred, the heroine, is trying to escape with her daughter across the border from America to Canada.

The wrong end of a telescope

I'm running, with her, holding her hand, pulling, dragging her through the bracken, she's only half awake because of the pill I gave her, so she wouldn't cry or say anything that would give us away, she doesn't know where she is. **The ground is uneven, rocks, dead branches, the smell of damp earth, old leaves, she can't run fast enough, by myself I could run faster, I'm a good runner. Now she's crying, she's frightened, I want to carry her but she would be too heavy. I have my hiking boots on and I think, when we reach the water I'll have to kick them off, will it be too cold, will she be able to swim that far, what about the current, we weren't expecting this.** *Quiet*, I say to her angrily. I think about her drowning and this thought slows me. Then the shots come behind us, not loud, not like firecrackers, but sharp and crisp like a dry branch snapping. It sounds wrong, nothing ever sounds the way you think it will, and I hear the voice, *Down*, is it a real voice or a voice inside my head or my own voice, out loud?

I pull her to the ground and roll on top of her to cover her, shield her. *Quiet*, **I say again, my face is wet, sweat or tears, I feel calm and floating, as if I'm no longer in my body; close to my eyes there's a leaf, red, turned early, I can**

see every bright vein. **It's the most beautiful thing I've ever seen. I ease off, I don't want to smother her, instead I curl myself around her, keeping my hand over her mouth. There's breath and the knocking of my heart, like pounding, at the door of a house at night, where you thought you would be safe.** *It's all right, I'm here*, I say, whisper, *Please be quiet*, but how can she? She's too young, it's too late, we come apart, my arms are held, and the edges go dark and nothing is left but a little window, a very little window, like the wrong end of a telescope, like the window on a Christmas card, an old one, night and ice outside, and within a candle, a shining tree, a family, I can hear the bells even, sleighbells, from the radio, old music, but through this window I can see, small but very clear, I can see her, going away from me, through the trees which are already turning, red and yellow, holding out her arms to me, being carried away.

Margaret Atwood (from *The Handmaid's Tale*)

Look closely at how the language of this extract creates tension. Study the features of the language by writing your answers to the questions that follow.

a   What happens in the extract?
Give your impression of the story, its setting and theme.

b   Much of this extract is written in small sections, or clauses. Rewrite the first section in bold print, using full stops instead of commas. Then, read the original sentences aloud, followed by your new version.
Why do you think Margaret Atwood has chosen to write in this way?

c   The extract is written in the present tense, as if it is happening as you read it. Rewrite the second section in bold print, as if it had happened in the past. Compare your version with the original. What difference would it have made to the passage if Margaret Atwood had used the past tense?
Why do you think Margaret Atwood has chosen to write in this way?

d   The writer did not need to include all the details in this passage in order to make her readers understand what is happening.
Why do you think Margaret Atwood included Offred's thoughts about her boots and the red leaf?

e   Margaret Atwood does not use speech marks in this extract. Why do you think that the few spoken words in this passage are in italics rather than the more usual quotation marks?

... on using language to make writing exciting

Try using some of the following techniques:

 Short sentences or clauses
These:

- create a sense of things happening quickly;

- make the reader move from detail to detail as an excited mind might;

- help the reader to move quickly through the passage.

 The historic present
This is where present-tense writing creates the impression that things are happening here and now.

 A different point of view
Examples of different points of view are:

- a first-person, or 'I', narrative that gives what you write the flavour of an eye-witness account;

- a third-person narrative – this is particularly useful when you have a complicated situation to describe.

 Comparative description
Comparative description is when you use similes or metaphors to build up an atmosphere that your reader may never have experienced.

 Understatement
Understatement is when unpleasant events are described in a flat – almost boring – way to add to their impact.

Writing a commentary

The extract below is taken from *Blood Shot* by Sara Paretsky. A detective, V I Warshawski, has been threatened about her involvement in a case she is investigating.

Read the extract carefully.

Between boulder and water

The trio of slickered fishermen had been watching my approach. They didn't seem to be doing much fishing. In fact, they didn't seem to have any gear. As I came to the end of the sea-wall they got up and formed a casual barrier between me and the road. A lone jogger passed behind the men.

'Hey!' I called.

The runner was deep in his Sony earphones. He paid no heed to us.

'Give it up, girlie,' one of the men said. 'We're just fishermen stopping a pretty girl for the time.'

I was moving away from them, trying frantically to think. I could head back up the sea-wall to the lake. And get trapped between boulder and water trying to get past someone's Walkman for attention. Maybe if I went sideways –

A shiny black arm swung out and grabbed my left wrist. 'The time, girlie. We'll just look at your watch here.'

I swung quickly in the circle of his arm, bringing myself in and chopping hard, upward on his elbow. He was well padded with slicker and sweater, but I got enough on the bone that he grunted and loosed his grip. As his fingers slackened slightly I wrenched myself free and tore off across the park, yelling for help. None of the few people who'd ventured out in the mist were close enough to hear me over their earphones.

I usually just follow the sea-wall in and out. I didn't know this stretch of the park, what hiding places it might hold, where it would take me. I hoped to land at Lake Shore Drive, but I might be dead-ending on a driving range.

My assailants were weighted down by their heavy clothes. Despite my fatigue, I put some distance between us. I could see one of them working his way across to my left. The other two were presumably coming around the top, trying to set up a pincer. It all depended on how fast I could reach the road.

I put out a burst of energy, cutting at an angle to the direction I'd been going. I'd surprised the man I could see – he gave a shout of warning to the two I couldn't. It gave me confidence and I started running all out. I was going at top speed when I saw water in front of me.

The lake. It stuck a finger into the park here. The end of the inlet lay about thirty yards to my left. The man I'd hit had moved down there, blocking my exit. On my right I could see the other two slickers, moving behind me at a casual jog.

I waited until they were within fifteen yards, getting my breath, getting my courage. When they were close enough that they could start calling to me – 'It's no use running – Give it up, girlie – No point in fighting' – I jumped.

The water was nearly ice. I took in a frozen filthy mouthful and spat. My lungs and heart banged in protest. My bones and head began to ache. My ears rang and light spots danced in my eyes. Yards. It's only yards. You can do it. One arm after the other. One foot up, one down, don't worry about the weight of the shoes, you're almost across, you're almost out, there's a boulder, slide across it, now you can walk, now you can climb up this bank.

The drawstring on my warm-up pants gave up completely. I wrestled myself free of them and lumbered toward the road. The wet cold was making me dizzy; inky shapes floated in front of me. I couldn't focus, couldn't see if the man at the bottom of the inlet had been able to move across the end before I'd swum over, couldn't see the size or shape of my pursuit. In my wet shoes, with my teeth chattering, I could hardly move, but help lay ahead. I pushed myself doggedly.

I would have made it if it hadn't been for the goddamn boulders. I was just too tired, too disoriented, to see. I tripped over a giant rock and fell heavily. I was taking great gasps of air, trying to get to my feet, and then I was writhing in black-slickered arms, kicking, flailing, even biting, when all the floating inky spots gathered into a giant ball and fire exploded in my brain.

After a time I knew I was very sick. I couldn't breathe. Pneumonia. I'd waited outside in the rain for my daddy. He promised to pick me up during a break on his shift, and the break didn't come – he never thought I'd wait that long. Lie under this tent, breathe slowly, watch for Mama, she says everything will be all right and you know she never lies. I tried opening my eyes. The movement stabbed great fingers of pain into my brain, forcing me back into darkness.

I woke again, rocking helplessly back and forth, my arms tied, a boulder pushing into my side. I was wrapped in something heavy, something that pushed into my mouth. If I threw up, I'd suffocate myself. Lie as still as possible. Not the time to struggle.

I knew who I was this time. V I Warshawski. Girl detective. Idiot *extraordinaire*. The heavy stuff was a blanket. I couldn't see, but I imagined it – green, standard Sears issue. I was wedged against the backseat of a car. Not a boulder, but the drive shaft. When I got out of here I'd get City Council to make front-wheel drive mandatory for all Chicago criminals. Get stopped with a drive shaft in your car and you'd do time, like the IRS getting Al Capone. When I got out of here.

My slickered friends were talking but I couldn't make out their words through the buzzing in my ears and the thickness of the blanket. I thought at first the buzzing was left over from my cold-water bath, but by and by my tired brain sorted it into the sound of wheels on the road coming through the floorboard. The rocking and the warmth of my cocoon sent me back to sleep.

I woke up to feel cold air on my head. My arms were numb where they'd been tied behind me, my tongue thick with suppressed nausea.

'Is she still out?'

I didn't know the voice. Cold, indifferent. The voice of the man who'd called in the threat? Only two days ago? Was that all? I couldn't tell, either of time or the voice.

'She isn't moving. Want me to open her up and check?' A black man's thicker tones.

'Leave her as she is.' The cold voice again. 'An old carpet we're dumping. You never know who may see you, even down here. Who might remember seeing a face.'

I kept myself as limp as possible. I didn't need another blow to the skull. I was pulled roughly from the car, banging my poor head, my aching arms, my sore back,

on the door, clenching my numb fingers to keep from crying out. Someone slung me over his back like an old roll of carpet, as though a hundred and forty pounds was nothing to him, as though I was nothing more than a light and careless load. I could hear twigs snapping underfoot, the swishing of the dead grasses. What I hadn't noticed on my previous trip here was the smell. The rank stench of putrefying grasses, mixed with the chemicals that drained into the marsh. I tried not to choke, tried not to think of the fish with their rotting fins, tried to suppress the well of nausea that grew with the pounding in my head as it bounced against my bearer's back.

'Okay, Troy. X marks the spot.'

Troy grunted, slid me from his shoulder, and dropped me.

'Far enough in?'

'She isn't going anyplace. Let's split.'

The rank grasses and soft mud broke my fall. I lay against the chill earth. The cool mud soaking through the blanket brought a moment's relief to my sick head, but as I lay there my body's weight caused water to ooze up through the mud. I felt the dampness in my ears and panicked, thrashing uselessly. Alone in this dark cocoon, I was going to drown, black swamp water in my lungs, my heart, my brain. The blood roared in my head and I cried tears of utter helplessness.

Sara Paretsky (from Blood Shot)

Write a commentary on this piece of writing, explaining what makes it exciting.

In a commentary, you try to identify the features of the writing that make it successful and appealing to a reader. Follow the steps for success on page 146.

Step 1

Read the extract through several times

As you read, make rough headings and jot down points. To help you get started, make a copy of the chart below on to a larger sheet of paper.

Points to think about	Things to look out for	Examples from this extract
Writer's stance	– who tells the story – how that person feels about events and characters – what his or her mood is	
Setting	– what you learn about previous events – the picture given of the surroundings	
Structure	– how the build-up, climax, release and pace are used	
Language	– any interesting choice of words, sentence structure and punctuation – any use of conversation	
Style	– whether it is descriptive or deliberately matter of fact	

Step 2

Decide on an order of importance for the points you have listed

Ask yourself which features contribute most to the success of the writing. If you are using the chart, number them in the final column.

Step 3

Write the first draft of your commentary

Start with an introduction explaining what the story is, what it is about, where it is set and what happens in the extract you have studied. Then, write a draft paragraph for each point you want to make. Leave plenty of space between the paragraphs.

Step 4

Add evidence and examples

Look back at the extract and find good examples to back up the points you are making. Either quote your examples or describe situations in your own words.

Step 5

Add a conclusion that sums up your views of the extract

Check back to see that you have made the important points in your notes and that you have supported them with examples.

Step 6

Revise and proof-read your writing carefully

Check spelling and punctuation. Check the quotations in particular.

Step 7

Write a final version for your coursework portfolio

... on using quotations in writing

There are many occasions when you want to use a quotation from a book in your own writing, and there are different ways of doing it.

If the quotation is quite short, make it part of a sentence:

> As she dives into the lake, the water is 'nearly ice'. The 'frozen filthy mouthful' that she takes in shows how unpleasant the lake is.

For a longer quotation, use a new line and a colon (:) at the end of the line before it. Indent (leave a space between the writing and the margin) the quotations:

> Sara Paretsky makes the reader feel involved with what is happening. As Warshawski comes round, she describes her feelings as they come to her, and the references to mouth, arms and tongue make them more vivid for the reader:

>> 'I woke again, rocking helplessly back and forth, my arms tied, a boulder pushing into my side. I was wrapped in something heavy, something that pushed into my mouth.'

>> 'I woke up to feel cold air on my head. My arms were numb where they'd been tied behind me, my tongue thick with suppressed nausea.'

If you are commenting on more than one book, a selection of poems or a non-fiction book, you should include a reference to show where the quotation comes from. For example:

> (*English Solutions* Book 4, page ...)
> (*Blood Shot* by Sara Paretsky)

4 Write in an exciting way

Plan some writing of your own. You do not have to tell the whole of a story but you should aim to write a scene which has a definite setting, a slow build-up, a main event and some description of what happens afterwards.

Make notes on the story you want to tell, the characters involved and the place where the events will happen. Make a chart like the one below and fill in details about the main sections of your writing.

Build-up	Climax	Release	A new build-up
On holiday in Slovenia my boyfriend has disappeared. Clues have led me to Castle Dread. My writing starts where I am searching the castle room by room; it includes lots of details – sights, sounds and smells!	My meeting with the vampire, Countess Bakwartz. Her death ... Discovery of boyfriend locked in tower.	Our escape from Castle Dread and our return to normal life.	My boyfriend has a new job – working nights!

When you reach the climax of your story you will want to make it as vivid and powerful as possible. Try one or more of these techniques:

- writing from different points of view;
- using long clauses and sentences;
- using short clauses and sentences;
- using different tenses.

Discuss the different versions with a partner. Decide which approach works best in your writing.

Now write the story. As you write, think about:

- varying the pace in the different sections of the story;
- making sure that the build-up gives enough background information for your reader to understand what is happening;
- making the release section a satisfying conclusion to the episode, *unless*
- deciding to finish the story on a new build-up of tension.

Save the final version for your coursework portfolio.

Language in use

ADDING DESCRIPTION

Adjectives are words that describe or modify a noun. They usually go in front of a noun but their effect on a reader can be changed by:

- altering their place in a sentence (for example, 'The gun, *black* and *menacing*, was pointed straight at him' or '*Rotten* and *stinking*, the zombie was crawling from the tomb.')

- using them in strings or linking them together (for example, 'they were hit by a rush of *hot, fetid* air as they entered the final chamber', 'the *blood-red* hand lifted the knife again')

Adverbs are the words that describe or modify verbs. Adverbs usually go after a verb, but their positions can be changed in similar ways to adjectives for effect:

Rapidly, he washed the blood from his hands. He *cautiously* and *noiselessly* turned the key.

Comparisons make events seem more real to a reader. They connect what he or she has probably never experienced to something that is familiar:

The zombie stumbled towards them, swaying *like a drunken man.*

Greg found it hard to breathe. He felt *as if he had just run a sprint,* not seen a murder.

Punctuation has an important function in descriptive writing, where it controls the pace of the writing. It can build up tension, add speed to a story's climax, or slow the pace of release. For example:

I had been driving for an hour or so. The road twisted and turned through the dark trees and there were precipitous drops to one side where the mountain fell away. My eyes felt heavy and my arm ached from the fight with the alien, and all around me was the pitch blackness of a star-less night.

Suddenly, an alien was in the road. It hurtled towards me. I swung the wheel as it clawed the windscreen. Its eyes were red and mad. The glass suddenly shattered. The car swerved violently. Everything went black.

When I came to, I was upside down in the darkness. It was deathly silent except for the hiss of a burst radiator and the tinny voice of the radio. The car was a wreck, but at least I had escaped the aliens once again.

After completing this unit, could you:

- give advice to a younger class on how to liven up their writing?

- discuss the techniques used in an exciting piece of writing in a book you are studying?

- write a commentary on your writing, explaining how you tried to make it varied and interesting?

on target

Language glossary

The words listed here all appear in this book and are all used in English lessons.

This glossary helps you to understand what these words mean and gives you an idea of how you can use them.

The word		What it means
accent	=	the way in which words are pronounced. Accents change from region to region, but the introduction of travel and television means that the differences between them are becoming less obvious. All languages are spoken with a variety of accents.
adjective	=	the describing words which modify the meaning of nouns. An adjective usually (but not always) goes in front of a noun in English.
adverb	=	verbs describe actions. Adverbs are describing words that modify the meaning of verbs. An adverb usually (but not always) goes after a verb and ends in -ly. Adjectives answer the question 'How?' about verbs.
adverbial clauses and phrases	=	clauses and phrases that act like adverbs to qualify a verb but are made up of groups of words. *Examples: 1 I am working so that I can buy a bike . 2 I am working until lunchtime .*
annotating	=	the practice of making notes on pieces of writing to help a reader. Shakespeare's plays are often annotated and students will annotate their own work as they redraft it.
apostrophe	=	a punctuation mark that shows contraction – where a word is shortened – or ownership – where one noun 'owns' another. *Examples: 1 I'm, we'll, they're 2 a flower's stem, the flowers' scent*
audience	=	the people who listen to what you say or read your writing. Your audience may be people you know, or people you do not know. You have to think about who your audience will be as you plan what you want to say.
brackets	=	also known as parentheses, brackets are placed around information that is separate from the main message of a sentence. Taking the words in brackets out of the sentence should not change its meaning.
clause	=	a group of words that make sense on their own usually separated by commas. In a sentence the main clause can make complete sense on its own. Subordinate or dependent clauses give extra information in a sentence but cannot stand alone.
closed questions	=	questions that have one obvious or clear answer. 'How old are you?'. 'Where do you live?' are examples.
colon	=	a punctuation mark used to show that lists or quotations will follow, or to divide a sentence where the second half explains or summarises the first. *Examples: 1 We have three cars in our drive: a Toyota, a Rover and an MG. 2 My life has changed for the better: I have a job, a cat and a wife.*

The word	What it means
comma	= a punctuation mark used within sentences to separate one group of words from another in ways that make the meaning of the sentence clearer. *Examples: 1 The suspect wore a green shirt, blue jeans and trainers.* *2 When the train came in, I jumped aboard.*
conjunction	= a word that links and adds meaning to sentences or clauses. 'And', 'but' and 'or' are the best known examples.
consonant	= any letter in the alphabet that is not a vowel. There are twenty-one consonants and five vowels in the English alphabet. You will find a consonant sound at the beginning or end of most words.
Creole	= a language dialect (often a mixture of two languages) that has then become the mother tongue, or main language, of an area.
dash	= a punctuation mark used to show a dramatic pause or an explanation. Dashes are used in direct speech to show where someone is interrupted. *Examples: 1 His handwriting is awful – yet he writes beautifully.* *2 'He's handsome,' said Jane, 'but he's also–'* *'A cad?' asked Quentin.*
dialect	= a variety of the language of a country. A dialect has its own words (vocabulary), word order and grammar. It is often connected with one particular region. In English, many regional dialects are used in speech, but most writing uses standard English. As with accents, the differences in dialects are becoming less obvious.
direct speech	= using people's actual words in stories in order to make them more realistic. Direct speech is usually placed within speech marks.
exclamation mark	= the punctuation mark (!) that shows when the preceding word has an extra emotional meaning. Exclamation marks are common in headlines, advertising and where direct speech occurs in stories.
first person	= writing a story using 'I', as if you were really in the events you are describing. The first person can bring a story to life or make a speech sound more heartfelt and convincing. It is almost always used in autobiography, where you write about yourself.
full stop	= a punctuation mark that shows the end of a sentence that contains a statement. Exclamation marks show the ends of sentences that give commands, show surprise or interrupt. Question marks follow questions.
future tense	= writing about the future, often using the words 'will' and 'shall' in front of a verb.
hyphen	= a punctuation mark identical to a dash but used to link words together. *Examples: plate-glass, well-balanced.*
noun	= words which name objects, places and things. Proper nouns are the names for people and places that begin with a capital letter. Abstract nouns describe things that cannot be observed or measured. Concrete nouns , as their name suggests, describe things that can. *Examples: 1 Jim, Geneva, Ferrari 2 Beauty, truth, ugliness 3 horse, brick, vegetable.*
paragraph	= a group of sentences that are linked together by their meaning. Paragraphs often start with the first word slightly indented. Otherwise there is often a blank line between paragraphs.

Language glossary

The word		What it means
persuasive talk	=	talk using strategies like threats, entreaties and repetition designed to make the listener change his or her mind.
phrase	=	a group of words that are connected but do not make sense on their own.
prefix	=	part words like 'dis-', 'anti-', 'un-', 'tele-', that go in front of words to change their meaning.
preposition	=	the word or words that come before nouns answering the questions 'Where?' and 'When?'.
present tense	=	writing about things as if they are taking place at the present time. The present tense is used for descriptions and in factual writing.
pronoun	=	short words that take the place of nouns in sentences. The main personal pronouns are 'I' and 'me', 'you', 'he' and 'him', 'she' and 'her', 'we' and 'us', 'they' and 'them'. Possessive pronouns identify ownership – 'mine', 'yours' and so on.
purpose	=	the reason why you are writing, or talking. Understanding what your purpose is helps you to shape your writing and make decisions about length and the level of vocabulary to use.
question mark	=	the punctuation mark (?) that shows when the preceding phrase is asking a question. In reading aloud, a question mark can change the way that a sentence is spoken.
quotation marks	=	punctuation marks also called <u>inverted commas</u> used to show the words that are spoken by somebody or 'quoted' from other writing. *Examples: 'I first realised that he was a bounder when I saw him trying to act in "Romeo and Juliet". He kept forgetting his lines.'*
register	=	a way of describing how people speak as opposed to what they say. People *modify* the register according to where they are and who they are talking to.
rhetorical questions	=	a question used for effect, often in speeches, which is not meant to be answered.
scanning	=	reading a text to search for information on a particular subject.
semicolon	=	a punctuation mark used to separate closely related but independent statements, to emphasise a contrast, or in lists. A semicolon has less effect than a full stop. *Examples: There are eleven players in a football team; in rugby there are fifteen.* *There are three reasons why you ought to be sent home from school: your late arrival at school each day; the absence of your homework; and the way you addressed Mr Crumb, the caretaker, as parrot face.*
sentence	=	a group of words which make sense when written on their own. Sentences begin with a capital letter and end with a full stop, a question mark or an exclamation mark.
skimming	=	reading a text to get the gist of what it is saying and to understand what it is about in general terms.
slang	=	the use of informal words, bad language or shortened words in speech or writing. Often, slang has its own rules or its own vocabulary.

The word		What it means
standard English	=	the dialect of English that is accepted as the correct form for writing in English. People who speak a regional dialect at home often speak standard English in formal situations.
suffix	=	part words like '-ness', '-ment', '-ful', '-ing', '-ism', that go after words to change their meaning.
syllable	=	the parts of a word made up of combinations of sounds. Each new sound in a word is represented (re-pre-sent-ed) by a syllable.
syntax	=	how words are ordered into sentences in a language. In English, syntax says that adjectives usually go in front of nouns. The syntax in French says they should usually go after nouns.
third person	=	writing a story or an account as if you were watching from outside rather than taking part in the events. Many stories are written in the third person where the narrator seems to be describing what happened without taking sides.
verbs	=	words that describe actions.
vowels	=	the letters a, e, i, o, u. Vowels make more than five sounds because they can be combined in words.

Presentation glossary

The word		What it means
bold type	=	the special effect in printing where letters are made thicker and darker on the page for emphasis. **This is bold print**. It is used in this glossary to make you notice key words.
draft	=	the first (rough) version of a piece of writing. A draft is sometimes written as notes or a plan.
font	=	the name given to the typefaces used by word processors.
graphics	=	pictures, tables and diagrams that are incorporated into your writing.
icon	=	a small picture or diagram used regularly as a visual reminder for something.
italic	=	a common effect where the typeface is *slanted like this*. Italics are often used for titles, foreign words or words that are referred to somewhere else in a book.
landscape page layout	=	printing, or writing, on a page with the longest edge at the top.
layout	=	the arrangement of words, or words and pictures, on a page. You talk about layout mostly when you are writing about posters, magazines and leaflets or experimenting with desktop publishing.
logo	=	the icon used by a company to link its products together. A logo is a visual symbol chosen by a company (or other organisation) to represent its image.
lower case	=	a name for small letters like these that are not capitals (upper case).
point size	=	a way of measuring the size of a typeface. Headlines are often as big as 60 point type while this glossary is printed in 8 point. Bigger typefaces are easier to read but they take up more space on the page.
portrait page layout	=	printing or writing on a page with the narrow edge at the top.
presentation	=	the features of layout, neat handwriting and spelling that make writing attractive and easy to read so that it communicates its message more effectively.
proof-read	=	a final check on writing, for punctuation and spelling errors.
storyboard	=	a way of writing for film and television that shows what a viewer sees alongside the words and music that accompany the picture.
typeface	=	the shape of the letters used in print. The typefaces used by word processors are known as 'fonts'.
upper case	=	CAPITAL letters – often used for effect or for titles and headings.
word-processing	=	the term that covers the use of computers as tools for writing. Word processors give the user control over the fonts used, their point size and the layout of the page. Many have spell-checkers that correct simple mistakes. Desk-top publishing programs give the user more control over layout and allow pictures and graphics to be introduced.

Acknowledgements

We are grateful to the following for permission to reproduce copyright material:

Ashford Buchan & Enright for an extract from *The Great Bike Ride* by Nick Sanders; English & Media Centre for the poems 'Don't Interrupt' by Demetroulla Vassili and 'You Never Took Me' by Engley Stewart from *City Lines*; Faber & Faber Ltd for the poems 'You're' from *Ariel* by Sylvia Plath and 'Rondeau Redoublé' from *Making Cocoa for Kingsley Amis* by Wendy Cope; Faber & Faber Ltd and Penguin Books Canada Ltd for extracts from *We Are Still Married* by Garrison Keillor; Gaia Books Ltd for an extract from *The Gaia Atlas of Planet Management* by Norman Myers. Copyright Gaia Books Ltd, London 1985 & 1993; Victor Gollancz Ltd and Delacorte Press, a division of Bantam Doubleday Dell Publishing Group, Inc for an extract from *Toxic Shock* (UK title)/*Blood Shot* (US title) by Sara Paretsky; HarperCollins Publishers Ltd for an extract from pp172–174, *A Book of Traveller's Tales* by Eric Newby; Authors' agent for the poem 'Warning' by Jenny Joseph from *Selected Poems* (Pubd. Bloodaxe Books Ltd). Copyright © Jenny Joseph 1992; Joan Daves Agency on behalf of The Heirs to the Estate of Martin Luther King Jr. for an extract from *I Have a Dream* Copyright 1963 by Martin Luther King Jr, copyright renewed 1991 by Coretta Scott King; New Beacon Books for the poem 'I Am Becoming My Mother' from *I Am Becoming My Mother* by Lorna Goodison (1986); Authors' agent on behalf of Grace Nichols for the poem 'In My Name'. Copyright © Grace Nichols 1983. Reproduced by permission of Curtis Brown Ltd; Polygon for the poem 'The Choosing' from *Yesterday Today And Tomorrow* by Liz Lochhead; Random House UK Ltd for an extract from *The Handmaid's Tale* by Margaret Atwood (Pubd. Jonathan Cape); *Rex Features Ltd* for extracts from the article 'Your house in 2013' by Patrick Griffin from *The Sun* 12.8.93; the author, Daphne Schiller for her poem 'I had rather be a woman'; Times Newspapers Ltd for extracts from the article 'Adult student boom on the way' by Ian Nash and Neil Hutton from *The Times Educational Supplement* 26.9.94 © Times Supplements Ltd, 1994; Virago Press Ltd for the poem 'The Fat Black Woman Goes Shopping' by Grace Nichols; Virago Press Ltd and Random House Inc for extracts from *All God's Children Need Travelling Shoes* by Maya Angelou; Authors' agent for an abridged extract from *500 Mile Walkies* by Mark Wallington (Pubd. Arrow Books 1989).

We have been unable to trace the copyright holders of the following and would appreciate any information that would enable us to do so: an extract from *Encarta*; the poem 'Woman Enough' by Erica Jong; the poem 'From: Six poems for hospital workers' by Diana Scott from *One Foot on the Mountain: British Feminist Poetry 1969–1979* ed. Lilian Mohin (1979); extract from *Our Joyce* by Joyce Storey (Bristol Broadsides).

We are grateful to the following for permission to reproduce photographs:

The Bridgeman Art Library page 68; The Julian Cotton Photo Library pages 46, 115, 125 (bottom right), 130 (top right, centre below, below right); Franke UK Ltd page 98; Friends of the Earth page 114; The Ronald Grant Archive page 92; Sally and Richard Greenhill pages 10 (top), 11 (middle), 21, 82, 125 (bottom left); Robert Harding Picture Library page 76 (centre) (James Strachan); Hulton Deutsch Collection pages 16, 17, 20; The Hutchison Library page 76 (right); Images of Africa/David Keith Jones page 72; Impact Photos pages 8 (Jeremy Nicholl), 10 (below) (John Cole), 11 (top) (Yann Arthus-Bertrand), (below) (Alex McNaughton), 80 (Ray Roberts), 104 109 (Mark Cator), 125 (top right) (Chris Pillitz) (top centre left) (Brian Rybolt) (centre) (Ben Edwards) (centre right) (Simon Shepheard), 130 (centre left) (Rupert Conant) (centre) (Simon Shepheard); The Kobal Collection pages 134, 148–9; Magnum Photos page 124 (Costa Manos) (inset) (Steve McCurry); NEC UK page 97; National Advisory Council for Education and Training Targets pages 85, 86; Pepsi-Cola UK page 28 (top and bottom right), 29; Range Pictures Ltd page 18, 76 (top left); Rex Features page 19; Montse Stanley page 82.

Special thanks to Hakuhodo UK Ltd for supplyig NEC advertising material and Clarion Communications for Perrier and Vittel advertising products.

ADDISON WESLEY LONGMAN LIMITED
Edinburgh Gate, Harlow, Essex
CM20 2JE, England and Associated Companies throughout the world.

First published 1996
ISBN 0 582 23984 2

Designed by Pentacor PLC (Warren Kerley)

Illustrations by David Atkinson, Martin Hargreaves, Nick Hawken, Debbie Hinks, Paul Hess, Martin Jones, Warren Kerley, Karin Littlewood, Anne Magill, Stephen May, Peter Maynard, Andy Parker.

Project Editor: Andrew Steeds

Picture Research: Penni Bickle

Set in 10 pt, New Century Schoolbook, Linotron 300
Produced by Longman Singapore Publishers Pte Ltd
Printed in Singapore